THERAPIZE YOURSELF

Choose to Heal and Find Your Truth

A Step by Step Program to Bring Out the Best Version of You by Integrating the Mind, Body and Spirit

ISBN Paperback: 978-1-7370341-1-7
ISBN Electronic: 978-1-7370341-0-0

Library of Congress Control Number: 2021910889

WAIVER
The author of this book is not dispensing medical advice or prescribing the use of any technique as a solution for physical, emotional, or medical problems. Please seek the advice of a physician or other qualified healthcare professional for any medical or psychological situation. The author intends to offer general information and skill-building techniques to help you in your quest for emotional and spiritual well-being. If you use any of the information in this book, neither the author nor the publisher assumes responsibility for your actions.

A NOTE FROM THE AUTHOR
I want to take a moment to acknowledge that when we dig in and face ourselves, we are walking into the possibility of getting triggered by past hurt and pain that has been unresolved. As you move through your journey, if you begin to get triggered at any point, I want you to turn to the skills I share with you and the support you need from outside professional sources.

If you do begin to feel triggered, please STOP, put the book down, and refer to your list of professional resources, coping skills, or supports you have created.

If you feel highly triggered, have suicidal thoughts, or do not trust yourself to keep yourself safe, call 911, go to an emergency room, or contact the National Suicide Prevention Lifeline 800-273-8255, which is available 24 hours.

Printed in the United States of America.

Publisher: Carrie Leaf Press

Carrie Leaf, MS, LMFT
United States

www.CarrieLeaf.com

DEDICATION

This book is dedicated to every soul that has altered my course, in both positive and negative ways. These shifts have in turn led me to myself.

This book is especially dedicated to my husband, Jimmy, who by the nature of his genuine heart and high vibrations, often guides me in changing my course in radical, exciting ways.

Above all, this book is dedicated to my sons, Mason and Nolan Leaf, who have shifted my course towards myself in the most profound way and motivated me to put in the work necessary to be the best possible version of myself.

A special dedication also goes out to my step-children, Vincent and Alexis Leaf, for being wonderful additions to my life.

Finally, this book is dedicated to everyone I consider family. Without my family (and close friends whom I consider family), there is no one to show me where I need to grow. Without growth, I do not get to experience the most this life has to offer. Thank you for your joyful connections.

> *When patterns are broken, new worlds emerge.*
> —Tuli Kupferberg[1]

---

[1] Tuli Kupferberg, https://www.goodreads.com/quotes/57149.

TABLE OF CONTENTS

FOREWORD

I was at my lowest point of life in college. The long, windy, and cold Midwest winters did not make the weight of life any easier for me. There is one distinct winter where everything felt a little warmer for me, and I will tell you about how my life shifted after that winter.

Until that point in my life, nobody had given me a safe space to speak what I thought or felt. I bottled everything up and kept it mostly to myself. The only place where I could share my deepest thoughts was in the depths of my journal. The benefit of this is that daily writing practices gave me the skills needed to cope in the present. I became a bestselling author in the personal development and emotional wellness space in the future, and I believe it's because I practiced writing about it for over a decade.

Experiencing trauma can often trigger patterns later that act as coping mechanisms. My pattern was choosing to be silent when I had a lot to say and deciding to listen too much when I wanted to speak—which was me not choosing my fullest expression. This was the result of growing up with two alcoholics who were emotionally unavailable and abusive.

During one of those cold winters, a ray of warmth came in. I met Carrie while I was doing undergrad, and she was studying for her master's. As a football player, the sport was my outlet for my pain, trauma, and unresolved issues. Carrie knew that I was choosing to be quiet, silent, and reserved—a trauma response. So, she challenged me safely to see my light; she held a candle up for me so I could walk out of the dungeons of my story and my suffering.

At that time, society wasn't talking about mental health, but Carrie was. She would ask me every day, "How are you doing?" and "How do you feel today?" She asked me repeatedly until I gave her a genuine answer, and she wouldn't settle when I pushed her away. She made me answer complex questions about how I felt, how I wanted to heal, and who I wanted to become.

Carrie wasn't a clinician at this point, but her aura created a safety net, a warm place to share thoughts and ideas. When I think back to the coldest era of my life, I am comforted knowing there was a benevolent soul who always wanted to know how I was doing—not because she was ready to judge me, or to tell me I wasn't good enough—because she saw the light in me that I didn't see. Carrie was inviting me into my fullest expression, and that's what she's doing here in this book.

Carrie figured out how to ball up all of that energy and warmth—and now, over fifteen years of practice—into *Therapize Yourself*. I know how it feels to be in a dark winter, and when you see that warm light, it's soul-shifting. That is what *Therapize Yourself* is. It's that warm candle that's here to call us out of our dungeons.

As a man who now has healed all of those childhood traumas, someone who has become a nine-time bestselling author and a leader in the global mental health conversation, I can say with all of my heart that Carrie's voice in *Therapize Yourself* is timely, needed, and unique.

As I think about the young man who needed guidance, words, and healthy spaces to dive deeper into his subconscious mind, I see that *Therapize Yourself* is a tool that will meet those needs and will create a warm space for someone to heal.

Carrie gives us one of the safest invitations to intimacy possible in this book. She guides us down a path of trying to understand our family structures, ourselves, and the available behaviors that will give us love and healing.

Carrie does a masterful job teaching us about the integration of the mind, body, and spirit. One of my favorite parts of the book is when she invites us to examine our negative and limiting beliefs. One of the most potent qualities of this book—that separates it from other books in this genre—is that Carrie tells you, "Good job!" As a reader, it feels like you are sitting in her safe office with her as you talk about the healing that is available.

Therapize Yourself is an experience that creates genuine integration. It's an invitation to explore the deeper layers we run from so we can begin to acknowledge and love our life holistically. It's a fun book to read, with loving words, and it's a needed voice at this time in our culture.

– Sylvester McNutt III

PREFACE

This book was created out of my desire to help and reach even more people than the incredible individuals who walk through my office door.

This book is a "spilling out" of all that I want to share with the collective energy of all souls.

This book is my attempt to organize all the thoughts, feelings, and art that are created in session with my truly amazing clients.

This book is a cumulation of things I've learned, experienced, witnessed, and grown from.

This book is a sharing of the best of me that I have to offer the world.

This book exists in the hopes that it will reach and touch even a single soul in a positive way.

This book is for you. This book is here to help guide, push, and motivate you to do the work required to heal and be healthy. This book is for the new you.

NOTE TO READER

Welcome to the first steps of creating a brand new you! For your benefit, I have included Notes pages at the end of each chapter and at the end of this book so you can journal your experiences and track your progress as you move through the exercises. I wish you every success with transforming your life and becoming the *You* you dream of being. Happy journaling!

Whatever we plant in our subconscious mind and nourish with repetition and emotion will one day become a reality.
—Earl Nightingale

ACKNOWLEDGMENTS

Thank you to my husband, Jimmy, for being supportive in anything and everything I ever do, without an ounce of judgment. You allow me to be my true self in every shape and form that I show up as.

Thank you to Michael Ireland for holding my hand every step of the way and for answering a zillion and one questions.

Thank you to Kristen Wise and Maira Pedreira of PRESStinely for also holding my hand, answering a zillion questions, and being a comforting and supportive presence during the vulnerable steps towards visibility.

Thank you to Sylvester McNutt III for being a beautiful soul, a good friend, and an encouraging support.

Thank you to my clients, past, present, and future—you always inspire me.

—Carrie

> *Learn to read symptoms not only as problems to be overcome but as messages to be heeded.*
> —Gabor Maté[1]

Chapter 1
INTRODUCTION

Here I am, sitting in a beautiful church in a small town in Eastern Iowa. The sun is shining divinely through the stained-glass windows, and I'm watching the reflected colors dance on my skin. The colors and the light are so bright—too bright. I feel like crying, but I'm avoiding it at all costs. Why? Because in this charming church, a group of practitioners are being trained in EMDR therapy. Another psychotherapist is practicing EMDR on me, but I'm not engaged with her. I have every excuse: The echoing noise of the other students is distracting. I'm not good at doing therapy. The lights on the EMDR apparatus we're using are moving too fast—and anyway, what could I possibly have to work on? At this point in my life, I've completed grad school and I've been a practicing marriage and family therapist for several years.

I wasn't expecting this. I am the helper, the healer, not the one who needs help. Generally, I'm happy, so what should I talk about? I can't identify a major problem, so I figure: "Keep it light." I pick an annoyance ... my dating woes. There's a pattern developing in this area of my life

---

[1] Gabor Maté, https://www.goodreads.com/author/quotes/4068613.Gabor_Mat_?page=4.

... I keep picking the wrong guy, over and over. At twenty-seven-years old, I'm single. When I was living in New York City, being single was fine ... everyone was single. Getting tied down wasn't on the radar or even a topic of discussion. However, when I came back to Iowa in my mid-twenties, I realized that many of my old classmates had already been married, divorced, and/or had kids. Culture shock.

"Okay," I think, "I'll work on this annoyance, give my therapist-partner something to practice on. Who knows, I might even learn a thing or two. Or, at least it will entertain my practice partner, right?" (Little did I know that EMDR would change my practice—and my life.) Still, I'm resisting her. My mind goes blank. I feel bad. "I'm a terrible training partner," I think. "It must be hard working with me. I'll bet she regrets getting me for a partner." I'm not resisting her deliberately; it must be subconscious.

She keeps pushing. In a matter of minutes, the floodgates open. Suddenly, we are delving into a relationship with my ex-fiancé, which ended about six years ago. I'd rarely thought about him, and in fact, in my opinion, I'd dodged a bullet by getting out of the relationship. So why would that relationship resurface?

The therapist keeps pushing. The next thing I know, we're talking about my belief system around the relationship—a belief I didn't even know I had. Me, a licensed marriage and family therapist, oblivious to this deep-seated negative belief system hanging out in my subconscious mind. I realize I walked away from that relationship feeling like, "I'm a handful," "I'm hard to love," and "I'm not good enough." My throat feels tight, tense, like there's a cement ball blocking my airway. It's hard to breathe, hard to swallow. What is this voodoo magic called EMDR therapy?!

In this moment; I'm changed forever. The power of the process and its ability to bring to my conscious mind my subconscious stuff was, well, mind-blowing. My takeaway? How could I be so blind? How could I have walked around with this subconscious belief system for so long? This realization didn't help the "I can't trust my judgment" negative belief that was already swirling around inside me either. "Why and how?" I wondered. "Why am I so blind to my stuff?"

I've studied the world of psychology for the last eight years of my life. I've worked hard to differentiate my character and personality from those of my family of origin and to develop my own thoughts and beliefs about the world and who I am. I've pushed myself to grow, to learn the human mind, and to learn about myself. I have a great family, great childhood memories. I know I'm loved. So why would I feel this way about myself? I mean logically, I don't feel that way in my head. But apparently, emotionally and physically, I do. How weird is that? How can my brain tell me one thing, but my heart and my body tell a completely different story? Oh ... that's what I was always asking myself about the guys I dated. My gut and intuition said, "Run, girl, run." But my over-analyzing, empathetic, co-dependent self convinced me there were a million reasons to stay. No wonder I picked the wrong guy over and over: Subconsciously, I didn't stand a chance. On a subconscious level, I'm showing up in my life in a way that says, "I don't believe I deserve anything better." Whoa. I should stop doing that. Especially now that I know what I'm doing.

If only it were that easy. If only insight could change our deeply engrained belief systems and behavioral patterns. That EMDR session was a great breakthrough for me ... but now I knew I had to do the work to break free of those repeating patterns.

So, that's me. What about you? What's your deal, anyway? What are you stuck on? Why do you keep doing that thing you do over and over? Why don't you learn? What's holding you back? Maybe you're stuck in a toxic relationship or a dead-end job. Maybe you're stuck in depression. Maybe anxiety holds you back. Maybe you can't lose weight. Maybe you can't take a risk you desperately want to take because you're afraid. Maybe you can't get over an ex. Maybe you keep doing that same old song and dance with your mom, even though you're forty-two years old. Whatever your problem is, wherever you're stuck in life, there's a negative belief behind it. My superpower is helping you identify and eliminate that negative belief so you can move forward and upward in life, so you can show up the way you want to—not in the unhealthy way you keep showing up over and over again on "repeat."

The path to healing, personal growth, and finding how to function at your highest capacity can be rocky. Growth and healing don't happen on a linear path. There are a lot of ups and downs and back-and-forths—it's hard. But it *is* worth it. To function our best, to level up in life, first, we need to get grounded. We need to create a safe, solid launching pad for the bumpy (but worthwhile) journey to the healthiest version of ourselves.

As a psychotherapist, I hear myself repeating to my clients that, "Nothing worth having in this life comes easy. The things worth having take hard work." If you picked up this book to gain something of value in your life, get ready. Get committed. Prepare to be uncomfortable for a bit. *Dig in.*

Just like therapy does not give you answers, this book will not give you answers. Why? Because you already have the answers. Yep, I just pulled the Jedi mind twist on you. You already have the answers you are searching for! Not only that, you are the only one who has the answers. Mind blowing, right? It's simple, really. You are the expert on you. You are the only person with access to what's in your head, heart, and soul. Therefore, you are the only one who can find your truth. You are the only one that can allow healing to take place on a mental, emotional, physical, and spiritual level.

You're probably thinking, "Well gee, thanks Carrie, I'm super glad I bought this book for you to put it all back on me. If I had the answers, I'd have done something about my problem already."

I know, I know. That's why I said, "It's not easy." This book won't tell you what your deal is or exactly how to "fix" it, but if you commit to this journey you're on, and you put in the time, effort, and energy, this book can help guide you to the answers within you. The best part? Once you've found your answers, you'll realize you already knew your answers—and that what you needed was the journey. Boom.

Okay. I'll stop talking in riddles and stop dropping the mind-bending bombs on you now ... Hehe. C'mon, let's have some fun. If we can't laugh at ourselves, at life, at our mistakes, at our humanness, we'll end up as angry, uptight people. Bring humor along for this ride ... we all do silly things.

On a serious note, arriving at our answers means going on this journey and facing some tough stuff about ourselves. There's no way around it. If we want to heal and grow, we have to go straight through the thick of it. For those of you who have kids, that last sentence sent me off into the song "We're Going on a Bear Hunt." If you haven't heard it, watch it on YouTube. I'm not sure whether to say, "You're welcome," or "I'm sorry"—but the song makes a valid point. We have to go through it. We can't go around it. We have to face it head on and deal with it. We have to learn how to tap into our intuition about what our mind, body, and soul need in order to heal and move forward in life. Go ahead, set this book down ... and find the kid's song on YouTube.

Whatever your "it" is has most likely been there for a long time. It doesn't matter if it's relationships, career, family, addiction, weight-loss issues, anxiety, depression, etc. As cliché as it is, your "it" probably originated somewhere in childhood. This isn't the case 100% of the time, but often it is. So, just as it took time to become a problem, it will take time to resolve the problem. The time spent healing, however, does not have to be equivalent to the time it took for your pain to hit the saturation point. The time it will take to heal will depend on your level of commitment, your willingness to be uncomfortable and push through, and your approach to doing so.

Ready to dig in?

NOTES

NOTES

NOTES

NOTES

NOTES

> *It is when you lose sight of yourself, that you lose*
> *your way. To keep your truth in sight you*
> *must keep yourself in sight*
> *and the world to you should be a mirror to*
> *reflect to you your image; the world should be a*
> *mirror that you reflect upon.*
> —C. JoyBell C.[1]

Chapter 2
WHAT'S MY PROBLEM?

What if you already know what your "it" (problem) is? Great! However, if you haven't made some progress towards healing, then you probably haven't invited your "it" in and sat down with it at the table. I'll say it again: Insight alone does not create behavioral change. Have you ever had an "Aha" moment of insight about yourself? For example, have you realized already why you keep choosing *that type* of guy, why you can't stop overeating, or why you never ask for a raise at work? Perhaps you feel so empowered by knowing your "it" and your "why," you're determined to change. Perhaps you set out with ambitious intentions ... but nothing changed, and six months down the road you found yourself in the exact place you were before: You pick *that type* of guy again (even though you know better), you start working out and counting calories (but still binge on cookies and ice cream every night), you make a plan to talk to your boss (but never follow through). You're

---

[1]   C. JoyBell C., https://www.goodreads.com.

stuck. Not only are you stuck, you're mad at yourself because you know better but don't do better. This is because even if you know what your "it" is, you've likely been avoiding it for a long time, so it is big and scary to you. I use the following analogy with my clients:

Say you have a huge debt. Let's say, for the sake of this analogy, that you're late on your car payment. You know the bill is coming in the mail. You don't know what to do ... you don't have the money. You're terrified. You shut down. You don't check the mailbox ... you don't want to see that bill telling you how much you owe and that they're coming to take your car. If you don't get the bill, you don't have to face the problem directly. It's not real; you just shove it away (for now). You might feel good for a while because you're out driving your car, and life goes on as usual. However, in the meantime, you're having strange physical symptoms: neck pain, stomach pain, but you aren't sure why. The anxiety is building underneath so intensely that it's manifesting in health issues. Still, you're avoiding the problem. Now you're getting late fees—and eventually, your car really is repossessed. Now you can't get to work. You lose your job. Your credit is dinged and drops. You can't get a new car, apartment, house, etc. with poor credit. You have a huge mess on your hands—all because you wouldn't address your problem. What started as one problem (which you could have resolved quickly with a payment plan—had you opened the mailbox and made a phone call)—is now magnified. It's turned into MANY problems.

Avoiding problems does not make them go away. Stop doing this. Face your stuff. We all have stuff. It's not how much stuff we have that is the problem, it's how we handle and manage the stuff that makes the difference. "My life is a great success. I am happy because I avoid my problems and pretend everything is great," said No One, ever.

So, what will you get from this book? This book helps you assess your life and lay down the healthiest, most solid foundation for deep healing and growth. Along the way, you might tackle some surface level "issues" too. Bonus! Together we will cover all the first steps I walk through with every client when they come through my office door. These steps are necessary to get you a solid base from which you can feel comfortable and strong as you dive deep into your core issues. Having a healthy foundation gives you a solid footing, so you can tackle that which you will bring to the surface. There is a reason you suppressed certain feelings ... but those feelings didn't go away. They linger deep down inside and begin to boil ... and you're like a singing tea kettle, all steamed up and ready to blow.

It is likely that you picked this book up because, on some level, you can sense the steam rising around a situation in your life. Have you (or are you about to) hit your emotional suppression saturation point? Is it time to heal, grow, and live your best life? Why not do it before you boil over? Because let's be honest, that won't be pretty. Oh—and life is short, so stop wasting your precious time.

Why tackle the past in order to heal and grow? Because the past got you where you are now. It made you who you are. It created your worldview and your belief system about yourself. We all have past "stuff" that holds us back. People are people ... and that means we are human ... we make mistakes. Every single one of us makes mistakes. Even those "friends" you look at on social media that look "picture perfect" with their Pinterest-worthy vacations, homes, and cars. They make mistakes too; I promise you they do. So, even if you had (on paper) the happiest, healthiest, most picture-perfect upbringing ever in the whole wide world, you'd still have "stuff." Your parents are human. They did (or didn't do) things that may have left a negative impact on you. Or at least a perceived one. You are human, which means you interpreted and internalized things in a way that may have impacted you negatively. There's no way around it—it's just "what it is." We are human: crazy, beautiful, flawed ... and resilient. The struggle of suffering and the beauty of growth are all just a part of life. They are the Ying and the Yang of life, and we are better off accepting them, not resisting them.

Now maybe you believe you've dealt with your "stuff." Even so, you're stuck. What gives? It could mean you *thought* you dealt with your stuff (and perhaps you did, on some level), but really you just shoved most of it down far enough that you believed it was gone. I see this happen regularly. My clients will tell me something traumatic that happened in their past and then say, "But I'm over it." Three to five minutes later, as they tell more of their story, tears well up and they say: "I don't know why this made me cry."

I'm guilty of this too. Remember that ex-fiancé I told you about? Not only would I have said, "I'm over that relationship and all that it put me through," I would have said, "I'm proud of all the 'work' I did to heal." Ha! I lied! I lied to myself about my healing. I cheated too ... I took the easy way out and suppressed it. Don't get me wrong; I was over the guy. That's why I believed I'd healed. The guy never crossed my mind, but I wasn't over the belief system I'd developed in that relationship. I wasn't healed from what being in that relationship did to my self-esteem.

Here's another scenario I see when my clients think they've dealt with their stuff: They're telling me their story, and I can't find even a hint of soul in their eyes. It's a horrific story of abuse, and they tell it straight, stone-faced, without an ounce of emotion. That "skill" of detaching is a trauma response. They've detached from the memory; they've pushed down layers of pain.

My point is this: You have to dig up the past for many reasons. Therapy helps you go through your life with a fine-tooth comb, making sure you're clearing out all the junk. Maybe you thought you'd cleared it out—but really you just shoved it on a high shelf in the back of a closet that you never open. You forgot about it. Then, a year later (or five years later), you open that closet, and boom! There's the junk, tumbling down on your head, smacking you in the face, demanding you deal with it. The junk always comes back with a vengeance.

This book will help you deal with that junk. By picking up this book, you took a first step toward that closet door. Now, you've opened the door. Working with this book is like reaching up and sorting through the jumble that's fallen on your head and dealing with it, sorting through the junk piece by piece; making peace with it. That's what this book is. It's the wonderful feeling you get when you hire a professional organizer to come over and clean out, label, and completely reorganize a closet so it's a breath of fresh air every time you open the door. I have experienced this wonderful feeling (quite literally with my kitchen closet). I hired someone to help me. Worth every penny, let me tell you! Sometimes we just need help to get our life decluttered. There is nothing wrong with needing help. (Thanks Anne Ahmann!)[2]

What is this book *not*? It is not a substitute for therapy. Remember: The length of your healing and growth process depends on the approach you take. The process of therapy is always more than the sum of its parts. When you build a healthy, therapeutic bond with a therapist, and there is trust and comfort at the core, there is a powerful healing magic in that relationship. Using a good therapist can propel you quickly into deep growth; you'll make more progress in your healing than you might ever have imagined. Back to my closet analogy—I looked at my messy, yucky closet for an entire year before I called Anne for help. All I can say is: I wish I had called sooner.

I am a firm believer that every single person (I repeat: *every single person*) could and would be wise to benefit from therapy. In my Utopia, it would be a weekly requirement for everyone. By writing this book, I hope I can reach people who haven't yet stepped into a therapist's office. I hope I can help readers do a self-assessment, help them build a healthy foundation for growth and wellbeing. For those of you who have done some healing and growing already, I hope to guide you through a re-evaluation (or deeper evaluation) of *self*.

We change continually. From one day to the next, one month to the next, one year to the next, we become different people. Our problems at twenty-three years of age are gravely different from our problems at thirty-four (well, mostly, anyway). Doing a self-assessment can help us put our current "stuff" in perspective.

If you've got past stuff that needs to be cleared out, this book will help you prepare to change and grow so you can live your best life. Let's get started!

---

[2] Anne Ahmann, https://www.happyhealthyhomedm.com/about.

NOTES

NOTES

NOTES

NOTES

NOTES

> *It's not selfish to love yourself, take care of yourself,*
> *and to make your happiness a priority. It's necessary.*
> —Mandy Hale[1]

Chapter 3
ASSESS YOUR LIFE: THE BASICS

Past Therapy

"Great," you say. "Sign me up. I'm ready. Where do we start?"

Get ready for the "Twenty Questions" game (on steroids). The questions in the exercise below may seem unrelated, but I assure you they are not. The more pieces to the puzzle I get, the clearer the picture becomes.

The first thing I want to know is, "Have you done therapy before?" Perhaps that question applies to you, perhaps it doesn't. If it doesn't, we can alter the question: "Have you done self-help work before?" If your answer is "No," welcome. Pat yourself on the back for being ready, willing, and able to begin, and please answer questions 5 and 6 below.

If your answer is "Yes" (to having had therapy in the past and / or to having done a self-help book, program, etc.), please take a few minutes to fill out the Therapeutic Experience Assessment below and share

---

[1] Mandy Hale, https://www.goodreads.com/quotes/7604845.

some takeaways from your experience. Sometimes writing things down pushes us—to think harder and to search deeper for an answer than if we are just reading along passively. So, pause now. Show yourself you're worth the time and effort to fill out the assessment below. Seriously. Fill it out.

Exercise: Past Therapeutic Experience Assessment

1. What are the top three takeaways from your previous therapy or self-assessment experience?

_____

_____

_____

_____

2. What did you enjoy about the process?

_____

_____

_____

_____

3. What did you not enjoy about the process?

_____

_____

_____

_____

4. How did the therapy or assessment change your life at the time?

_____

_____

_____

_____

5. If you have never done therapy or self-help in the past, why not?

_____

_____

_____

_____

6. Space for your own questions/observations/free-flow thinking:

_____

_____

_____

_____

If you completed the assessment above, good work! If you didn't, I will know. Just kidding—I won't know. You won't get into trouble … but you will get back what you give. If you couldn't be bothered to fill out one page of questions, do you think you can put in the work required to change your life? Let's be real here, right?

Medical History

Next, I want to know about your medical history. Are there any major illnesses or do you have medical history I should know about—surgeries, broken bones, etc.? I want to see if there are medical issues that influence your daily life, your mood, or your quality of life. If so, I want to know how you are managing these. What medications are you on, if any? Are they working? Are there side effects? This information is important. If you are having problems with current meds, for example, it is important to assess whether you are on the right dose, if a good provider is prescribing those meds, etc. Before we dig deeper, we want to get these things balanced out and managed well. If you are on meds, I want to know that you trust your provider, that you can tell them everything that's going on. If your diagnosis is complex, I want to see you with a psychiatrist (as opposed to a primary care physician). If you, your provider, or I (as your therapist) are on the fence about your diagnosis, I will probably want to send you to a psychologist to get testing done for an accurate diagnosis. For example, we don't want to be "barking up the wrong tree" for six months, only to find out that what we thought was a mental health issue was a physical health issue. Often, symptoms of mental health can overlap and look like something else. For example, depression symptoms may actually be anxiety and vice versa.

Perhaps you're not on meds ... but you would benefit from being on them. Personally (and clinically), medications are a last resort. I like to take a holistic approach and see if we can tackle issues organically. However, there are times when meds are needed—and when they work, they can be life changing. I give this a three- to six-month window, waiting it out and working organically through therapy, before turning to meds. There are variances in this time frame, of course, depending on the severity of symptoms and the amount of progress a client is making (or not making). If someone cannot get themselves out of bed and to work, for example, we will probably look to meds sooner than we would with someone who's feeling mild, circumstantial symptoms of depression. If you are facing medical issues and you have no explanation for your symptom set, or have not consulted a medical professional, I will recommend, foremost, that you visit your primary care physician to rule out anything we may be missing.

As cases in point, I'd like to share a few examples involving medical issues that have stood out in my practice. In one case, in my first year out of grad school, a teenage boy came to therapy to work on trauma issues. This boy had been jumped by a group of kids and had feared for his life. But the symptoms he reported and his lack of progress didn't seem to match up. I was at a loss and confused; his progress was minimal. His moods and what his mom reported were not in accord with what he shared and talked about in session. He was a tall, thin, healthy young man and reported no major medical issues. His mom shared her frustrations with me, reporting that her son drank up to seven pops a day. She saw this as defiance and disrespect as she had asked him to limit his pop intake. He had no excuse other than "being thirsty." After some time, he had a doctor's appointment in which they figured out he was diabetic. This was affecting so many things in his life: his mood, his eating/drinking habits, his focus and attention, his anxiety, etc. This was an eye-opener for me regarding the mind/body connection and why we need to look at all areas and how they affect each other in a client's system.

Another case that stands out was with a thirty-something-year-old man. At his wife's request, they were coming to me for couple's counseling. She shared her frustrations: "He never listens to me," she said, "never remembers anything, never follows through on anything." He responded that these things occurred because he was "probably ADHD" (self-diagnosed). His symptoms sounded like ADHD, but something felt out of place. I referred him to a psychologist for testing. The report came back: no ADHD. Instead, the psychologist diagnosed high anxiety and recommended meds and therapy. This proved to be a game-changer, both for the man and for his marriage.

A final example of the importance of knowing someone's medical history before a course of therapy begins was one that showed up the other way around: mental health causing physical symptoms. This client was an otherwise healthy woman in her forties, suffering chronic back pain. She was referred to me by an in-tune, holistic physical therapist.

This physical therapist had been working with her for a while and though progress had been made, they couldn't seem to eliminate all of her pain or understand why it was occurring. This client had never considered coming to therapy, but at this point in her struggle, she was open to anything. As we dug into an assessment, I learned of her history of physical and sexual abuse by a family member. She admitted she had never dealt with it and while she felt intense anger towards her perpetrator, she never expressed it. Instead, she held it all in ... for over thirty years. We began the EMDR process and by the end, her back pain became a non-issue.

The body holds our trauma. Addressing and ruling out medical concerns is an important part of laying a solid foundation for healing and growing. The mind/body/spirit connection is real and vital to overall health and wellbeing.

Substance Use / Abuse

The next step of the assessment process is to check in with you on your use of substances. First, I ask, "Are you using drugs? What about nicotine, caffeine, or sugar?" While people overlook these substances, they have a big impact on our mood and functioning. They can all magnify anxiety, cause us to "crash," or end up making us feel lethargic or irritable. So, if you are already anxiety-prone, adding nicotine, caffeine, or sugar on top of it isn't a great idea.

Once you've identified (or admitted to) using substances, it's time for the second question: "Are you abusing any of these substances?" Because answering this question can be hard for people to define or admit honestly, I start out with a discussion. If, for example, your drug of choice is illegal, I can't condone your use of it. Not only are you endangering your wellbeing, there are potential legal consequences. What the drug is doing to your brain and body is enough, never mind what a legal record for possession could do to your career, life, and future—it could be devastating and hard to dig out of. There is, of course, no judgment. Addictions can get the best of anyone. I repeat: Anyone! We all have vices; they just don't always show up in the form of drugs or alcohol.

When we look at your use of legal drugs, first we assess your average use. If we are talking about coffee, for example, are you having two cups a day or eight cups a day? Again, what is "healthy" will range from individual to individual and is debatable. According to the Mayo Clinic, up to 400 milligrams (mg) of caffeine per day appears to be safe for most healthy adults.[2] That's roughly the amount of caffeine in four cups of brewed coffee, ten cans of cola, or two "energy shot" drinks. If you are anxiety prone, I encourage you to cut the Mayo Clinic recommendation in half ... at least.

Alcohol dependence may not always be as obvious as one may think. We have to ask questions like, "What is your weekly average?" "What is your daily average?" Getting specific is necessary. For example, if you say, "I have a few drinks in an evening," are we talking two to three drinks in a sitting ... or ten to twelve? Are we talking about average-sized drinks, large drinks, or shots? Are we talking about wine, beer, or liquor? According to the Mayo Clinic,[3] moderate alcohol use for healthy adults means up to one drink a day for women of all ages and men older than age sixty-five, and up to two drinks a day for men age sixty-five and younger.

Examples of one drink include:

- Beer: 12 fluid ounces (355 milliliters)
- Wine: 5 fluid ounces (148 milliliters)
- Distilled spirits (80 proof): 1.5 fluid ounces (44 milliliters)

Of course, given these guidelines, we also have to factor in questions such as "Are you a healthy adult?" "Are there medical concerns you could be exacerbating?" For example, let's go back to caffeine. If you are struggling with high blood pressure, caffeine is worse for you than it would be for someone who does not struggle with high blood pressure.

---

[2] https://www.mayoclinic.org/healthy-lifestyle/nutrition-and-healthy-eating/in-depth/caffeine/art-20045678.

[3] https://www.mayoclinic.org/healthy-lifestyle/nutrition-and-healthy-eating/in-depth/alcohol/art-20044551.

Next, I want to know how these substances are influencing or affecting your life. Are people telling you that you have a problem? Are you fighting with a spouse over your substance use? Are you having trouble falling asleep or waking up? Are you showing up late to work? Have you had medical issues because of substance use? A common complaint I hear from spouses of those abusing substances is that their loved one experiences mood swings. So, if any substance is having a negative impact on your life, it *is* a problem for you. Sometimes, however, it is hard to know if our surface-level issues (such as falling or staying asleep) are because of abuse of a substance. (But sleep disturbance is a common side effect of most substances that we put in our bodies.)

After we look at the average consumption of your substance of choice and how it affects your life, I ask about your reasons behind your substance use: "Are you using substances socially?" "Are you using substances to celebrate, to relax, or to 'numb out'?" Together we examine your answers. Your reason for substance use plays a large part in how it affects you and how much you use as well. Again, this requires honesty.

Once you have been honest with yourself about your substance use, we decide: Is your current use healthy? Or do you need to make changes? Sometimes, before we can dig in to deeper-level issues in therapy, we need to give the process time and space so the client can bring their substance consumption to a healthy level. At other times, referrals to substance abuse treatment programs can be helpful. Why? Because substance use can hinder the growth process (if not impede it entirely). There is no way around the fact that if you are putting detrimental substances into your body, you are altering your state of mind. If you are not working with a clear mind, you are not working entirely with the truth—and to see progress in healing and growth, you need both a clear mind and the complete truth.

Once I had a client come in, wanting to work on himself in order to improve his marriage. The client was in his mid-forties, a clean-cut, well-put-together, high-functioning executive. We worked hard to figure out where we needed to start, what he needed to work on, etc. As we were digging in, we ran into some past traumas, so we needed to attend to those first. This client was committed and working hard. We discussed his drinking, how it might hinder his progress, and that we might have to put his therapeutic journey on hold until he could either cut back substantially or go through treatment. He admitted his relationship with alcohol was (perhaps) concerning and agreed to cut down. Throughout our time together, the client was honest: He was still drinking. He had cut down, wanted to cut down more, but was struggling. He said it wasn't impacting his life drastically; nevertheless, he wanted to work on it. Eventually, the story unraveled: He was drinking more than he was letting on, and it was causing major issues in his marriage.

At that point, we got him into an in-patient substance abuse treatment program, and then jumped back into therapy sessions. He completed the in-patient treatment and then started couple's counseling with his wife in addition to his own individual therapy. He has been sober for five years, continues to work on and rebuild trust with his wife, and is happy that he changed his life and is more present with his kids.

So, as you can see, drinking or drugs is never the *only* problem—beneath this client's drinking issues were unresolved trauma experiences he had suppressed most of his life. This bled out into his personal relationships. Once he got sober, he faced and worked on the trauma, dropped the heavy baggage he had been carrying for years, and mended his relationships and his life.

NOTES

NOTES

NOTES

NOTES

NOTES

> *Our thoughts are mainly controlled by*
> *our subconscious…and you cannot change*
> *the subconscious mind by just thinking about it.*
> *That's why the power of positive thinking will*
> *not work for most people.*
> *The subconscious mind is like a tape player.*
> *Until you change the tape, it will not change.*
> —Bruce Lipton[1]

Chapter 4
ASSESS YOUR LIFE: THE DEEP DIVE

In this section of the assessment, I ask about your Present-Day Living Environment. This includes your housing, your family, your job, your finances, your legal record, etc. This review may or may not bring additional problems to your list that you may have overlooked. I look at these issues for several reasons, a primary one being that if we can't meet our basic needs (such as buying groceries or paying our rent/mortgage), how will we have the space to take a deep dive into our wellbeing? This part of our review follows the idea of Maslow's Hierarchy of Needs.[2]/[3]

---

[1] Bruce Lipton, https://www.brainyquote.com/topics/subconscious-quotes.
[2] https://www.simplypsychology.org/maslow.html.
[3] https://support.shutterstock.com.

```
                    SELF-
                 ACTUALIZA-
                    TION
              morality, creativity,
            spontaneity, acceptance,
          experience,purpose, meaning
             and inner potential

               SELF-ESTEEM
      confidence, achievement, respect of others,
           the need to be a unique individual

            LOVE AND BELONGING
      friendship, family, intimacy, sense of connection

            SAFETY AND SECURITY
      health, employment, property, family, social ability

            PHYSIOLOGICAL NEEDS
      breathing, food, water, shelter, clothing, sleep
```

Maslow's hierarchy starts with *physiological* needs: air, food, water, sleep, and other factors that move us towards homeostasis. At this level are our basic needs—foundational essentials that we will want to meet before we move up to the next level. If we cannot get food and water, for example, we don't worry about anything else ... we are in survival mode.

The next level is *safety*. Safety includes the security of our environment, our employment, resources, health, and property, etc.

Next comes *belongingness*: love, friendship, intimacy, and family, etc.

After belongingness is *esteem*: confidence, self-esteem, achievement, and respect, etc.

Finally, at the top of the pyramid is *self-actualization*. This includes morality, creativity, and problem-solving, etc.

Addressing higher-level needs is much easier when we are in a place in our life where we don't have to stress or worry about lower-level needs. This is why we do an assessment of our environment—we are building our foundation (the bottom half of the triangle) in order to address the rest of our needs (the upper half of the triangle).

Therefore, I want to know: Where in this triangle are you at currently? What is going on in your day-to-day life? What consumes most of your time, energy, and thoughts? What are you missing from your foundation that may hold you back from addressing your higher-level needs?

Now it's time to push "Pause" yet again. Please fill out the questionnaire below. Your answers will help to identify your needs and the current status of your everyday environment. I want you to go environment by environment. Write down anything about each environment listed—the pros and the cons. Allow yourself to free-flow any thoughts and feelings that come up in each area.

Exercise: Environmental Scan

1. Memetic Environment – Ideas, books you read, podcasts you listen to, websites you visit, and all the information you consume.

_____

_____

_____

_____

2. Financial Environment – Your money, wealth, and budget.

_____

_____

_____

_____

3. Relationship Environment – Your close friends, family, and close colleagues.

_____

_____

_____

_____

4. Network Environment – Your professional connections, greater community.

_____

_____

_____

_____

5. Physical Environment – The places and things that surround you.

_____

_____

_____

_____

6. Body Environment – Your energy, appearance, and clothing.

_____

_____

_____

_____

7. Self-Environment – Your strengths, talents, and character.

_____

_____

_____

_____

8. Spiritual Environment – Your deep connections and sacred spaces.

_____

_____

_____

_____

9. Nature Environment – Your relationship with the great outdoors.

_____

_____

_____

_____

Once you have finished the Environmental Scan page, evaluate your answers. Did any new problems pop up? Are any of these stressors the cause of other problems you listed? Take your time. Are there stressors in your everyday life that you did not list in the "Past Therapeutic Experience Assessment Exercise" in the last chapter? Is there a transportation issue you overlooked, a current fight with your best friend, or a lack of friends, etc.? Think of your everyday life. Is there a recurring problem that pops up nearly every day? Take a minute to jot down any newfound issues in your life.

_____

_____

_____

_____

_____

_____

_____

Family History

Next up is the Family History section. Completing this section is vitally important for mental health because our issues are due to either "nature" or "nurture." Both can lead us back to the same location: our parents and our upbringing. What I mean by "nature" is biology, genetics, and hereditary issues. For example, are we the way we are because we are genetically predisposed to anxiety, depression, etc.?

"Nurture," refers to learned behaviors. Sometimes our nurture problems may be because of a small "t" trauma. For example, maybe we had available and supportive parents with a good upbringing, except one parent would make critical and judgmental comments often. Or, it may be a Big "T". For example, maybe we act out our anger through violence because that is what we saw mom do when she was upset. Or maybe you were in active duty and saw combat action—this is a nurture (learned) experience that may have led to PTSD symptoms.

Two different people can go through the same experience and have completely different responses. For example, maybe one person was genetically predisposed to anxiety, and the other wasn't. Or maybe one was brought up being taught healthy coping skills, and the other saw his or her parents drinking alcohol to cope. These factors make a big difference in the response we have—so we want to investigate and get an idea of why we do what we do.

First, I want to know if anyone in your family has a mental health disorder or substance abuse issue. This could be your parents, siblings, aunts, uncles, or grandparents. Often my clients will say "No" because no one in their family has been formally diagnosed. However, if we take a minute to look at things, we might realize, for example, that since her teens your aunt has experienced waves of depression. Similarly, maybe your dad is wound pretty tight and struggles with anxiety. These family issues can be hard to identify, so we may not be absolutely sure, but we want to note it. After all, we share a similar biological make-up with the members of our family unit.

Assessing your family background can also be helpful if you end up taking a medication. Often a medication that works for one family member will also work for you, so this can save us a lot of time going through the ups and downs of medication trials. If you end up needing medication, there is now testing (such as The GeneSight® test)[4] that can help determine what medication might work best based on your genetic makeup. This too can save time in the treatment process.

---

[4] https://genesight.com/.

Next, I want to understand your relationships with your family members. One by one, I want to hear the dynamics between each member of your immediate family. Or, if an extended family member was significant in your life, I want to know the relationship dynamics with them. When I look at family relationships, I want to know things like, "Are you close with that family member? If so, how close? Are you too close (which would be termed 'enmeshed'), or is there a healthy boundary there? Are you distant? If so, how distant, and why? Do you avoid each other, or is there a hard line drawn where there is no communication or relationship at all? Do you share deeper levels of your life with them? Whom do you turn to first? For what? Are you happy with the relationship with each family member? What would you change about the relationship, if anything?"

I also want to know what kind of person each member of your family is. For example, what do they do for a living? Are they kind, funny, busy, stuck up, materialistic, oblivious, loud, judgmental, reserved? Do they share feelings or bottle them up? Our family members rub off on us in many different ways. It's interesting and surprising to step back and see how one person's ways may have influenced our own ... without us realizing it.

Next, I want to know the whole family's patterns, boundaries, secrets, and dynamics. How does the family function as a whole? The sum is always greater than the parts, and there is an energy that exists within each family. This is called our *homeostasis*. Homeostasis is a balanced environment of the family—and a family will work automatically to maintain this internal, steady state.

You've got a homeostasis of your own. Think of it as your house's central air unit. You figure out a comfortable temperature for you, you set it, and the unit works automatically to keep your whole house at that temperature. The same is true for your broader family's homeostasis. In this homeostasis, there is a tendency for the family system to maintain this way of being at all costs, and there is a strong resistance to any change. This is why, for example, it can be extremely hard to get married and blend two families together, particularly if our way of being, our upbringing, and our habits and dynamics are way off from our partner's.

This is also part of the cause behind the struggle with differentiation of one's identity, values, and beliefs from those of your family of origin.

What does this mean? Well, a lack of differentiation from your parents or your past can influence your present-day behavior strongly. Family therapy pioneer Murray Bowen explains that healthy differentiation occurs when a person separates from their family to the extent that they can distinguish their emotions from those of their family members.[5] Differentiation is important in understanding yourself and who you are and in creating a healthy life, future, and family of your own. There is a lot to differentiation, and it is helpful in knowing where it plays a part in your everyday life. You'll delve more into this subject when you take that "deep dive" with your therapist into your family-of-origin issues.

Back to family dynamics. When I say "I want to know about the dynamics in your family," that may include things like, "What are the roles of each family member? Does your family use humor often or are they more serious? Are sports central to your family? Are traditions or religion strong in your family? Is anger an acceptable form of expression in your family? Does your family drink alcohol? Was there structure and routine when you were growing up?" The answers to all these questions help me understand how you developed your worldview and how these things contributed to the lens through which you look at the world. Your answers to these questions help define for me what does or doesn't make sense for you. Family dynamics are strong and have powerful holds on us—particularly when they are subconscious. We want to bring these issues to the surface, lay them out, examine them, and understand them. Then we can decide if they fit and if they make sense in the life we want—or if we need to cut some ties and challenge some beliefs.

---

[5] P.J. Jankowski and L.M. Hooper, "Differentiation of self: A validation study of the Bowen theory construct," *Couple and Family Psychology: Research and Practice* 1(3) (2012): 226–243, https://doi.org/10.1037/a0027469 and https://psycnet.apa.org/record/2012-05951-001.

_____

_____

_____

_____

_____

_____

_____

Trauma

Next, we look at if there has been any trauma in your life. A trauma is a deeply distressing or disturbing experience. Often "trauma" is in the eye of the beholder, but some Big T traumas include mental, physical, or sexual abuse, divorce, death/loss, seeing combat in active duty, or something like a serious car accident, natural disaster, etc. Any situation in your life in which you questioned whether you were going to die was likely traumatic—and those situations are at the top of our list to deal with. Sometimes there is a "Big T" (one large traumatic event) that leads to a symptom set, or there is an accumulation of a bunch of "little t's" over your lifetime (e.g., Mom and Dad fighting all the time, a parent who was critical of you, lack of stability as a child, etc.). We can also deal with consequences from trauma that occurred when you were preverbal. Perhaps, for example, you had a traumatic birth. I was born with the umbilical cord wrapped around my neck, which turned me as blue as a Smurf at childbirth (or so I'm told). Of course, I do not remember this, but it is highly likely that it has affected me. My first experience coming into the world was that of needing to fight for my life. I have always been a fighter, competitive, wanting to win, and a bit of a sore loser. Perhaps losing means death on a subconscious level to me. I wonder often how much of this is because of my birth experience.

The trauma that affects your life and wellbeing doesn't have to be your own. For example, perhaps your parents or grandparents went through trauma—that type of trauma is called "transgenerational trauma," and Wikipedia defines it as trauma transferred from the first generation of trauma survivors to the second and further generations of offspring of the survivors via complex post-traumatic stress disorder mechanisms.[6] This is why examining your family-of-origin history is so important when you are working on yourself.

Often, a trauma may be the entire focus of a therapeutic treatment plan (or, at the very least, it will be treated as the origin of a current problem). When it comes to having experienced trauma, the effects can show up in our lives as many symptoms, for many years down the road. There can be many triggers to these experiences—and they can be powerful. If you have experienced a trauma, I highly encourage you to participate in EMDR therapy. I use this therapy in my practice all the time for many problems, but definitely with trauma. The results I have seen with EMDR in my practice never cease to amaze me.

_____

_____

_____

_____

_____

_____

_____

_____

[6] https://en.wikipedia.org/wiki/Transgenerational_trauma.

Support System/Coping Skills/Strengths

Next, I inquire into your support system, your coping skills, and your strengths. For your support system, I want to know, "Who are your friends and confidantes? Whom do you trust the most? Whom do you go to with problems? Who helps lift you up?" I think many people would be surprised at the small circle of support most individuals have. Sometimes this is an area we work on in therapy, helping clients to strengthen relationships or build new support systems. This is not always easy to do, but it is often underrated or overlooked. For those of you with support systems already in place, I'm curious: Are you happy with them? How often are you seeing/talking to your supports? Do you get as much as you give? Would it be helpful to see/talk to your supports more? I have noticed that the older we get or the busier we get—and when we get married and have children—time for our friends and supports seems to dwindle and go on the back burner. This is often a tragic mistake for many individuals' wellbeing, because as human beings we thrive on connectedness. Even if you're an introvert, examine your social support network. Are you happy with it or not? Does it need some work? Where can you nourish and grow it?

_____

_____

_____

_____

_____

_____

_____

Next on the assessment roster is your coping skills. This area is huge. When I inquire about coping skills, an alarming number of people say, "I don't have any." When I do some digging, my clients can come up with at least one coping skill, but often it is a negative or unhealthy coping skill like drinking alcohol. To help us dig further, I ask, "What do you do when you're feeling sad, frustrated, angry, hurt, etc.? What is your go-to in order to feel better?" Unhealthy coping skills can be difficult to break, but we do not want to break them until we have some healthy ones to fill the gap. This is a trial-and-error process and because everyone's coping skills are different and because what works for you can change from day to day, it will take time to figure out what works for you. For example, one day, a long hot bath at the end of the day might be the ideal relaxation technique. The next day, your kids might behave like monsters and there is no time for a bath until well past bedtime. Therefore, you may need a quick five-minute coping skill to unwind from the chaos. I encourage clients to keep many coping skills in their tool boxes.

I often use the terms "coping skill" and "self-care" interchangeably. I encourage my clients to be "preventative," making sure they are doing self-care every single day. Fitting in self-care daily will help keep your stress threshold down. Picture yourself as that boiling tea kettle again, with water and steam sputtering out ... When you fit in self-care, you pop the lid and let some steam out ... so you don't boil over. The more often you let out the steam, the less chance there is of spill over into other areas of your life.

So, what do I mean by "self-care?" Self-care behaviors are those things we do that make us smile, laugh, relax, unwind, function at our best, feel happy, and generally just feel good. We need at least one act of self-care every single day or else we will deplete our mental / emotional / physical / spiritual reserve. It's time to push Pause again and evaluate your own coping skills and self-care techniques. Below is a list of a few healthy (and unhealthy) coping skills as well as some self-care ideas. Pick some from the healthy coping skills and self-care list to add to your own list. Take the self-care time to fill out the Exercise below.

Exercise: Exploration of Coping Skills and Self-Care

1. What is my go-to activity when I am angry and want to feel better?

_____

_____

_____

_____

2. What is my go-to activity when I am sad and want to feel better?

_____

_____

_____

_____

3. What is my go-to activity when I am lonely and want to feel better?

_____

_____

_____

_____

4. What is my full list of coping skills?

_____

_____

_____

_____

5. What are my daily self-care activities?

_____

_____

_____

_____

Examples of Healthy Coping Skills

- Exercising (running, walking, etc.).
- Writing (poetry, stories, journaling).
- Doing art/crafts/anything creative.
- Calling a friend/going to see a friend.
- Watching a funny movie.
- Listening to music.
- Painting your nails, doing your make-up or hair.
- Singing.
- Punching a punching bag.
- Crying.
- Taking a hot shower or a relaxing bath.
- Playing with a pet.
- Cleaning something.
- Reading a good book.
- Trying some aromatherapy (candles, lotions, room sprays).
- Meditating.
- Going somewhere public.
- Baking or cooking.
- Decluttering.
- Writing a letter.
- Doing yoga.

Examples of Unhealthy Coping Skills

- Drinking caffeinated beverages.
- Smoking.
- Drinking alcohol.
- Spending money.
- Eating emotionally.
- Avoiding problems.

Examples of Self-Care

- Developing a regular sleep routine.
- Aiming for a healthy diet.
- Using your sick leave.
- Getting some exercise.
- Journaling.
- Having a hobby.
- Unplugging from electronics.
- Making time to engage with positive friends and family.
- Saying "No" sometimes.
- Setting boundaries.

Now I would like to know about your strengths. What are some good things about you as a person? What are some things you are good at? These can be hard questions for people to answer—some people might be modest; others cannot think of any. It is not uncommon for clients to not come up with a single strength. We can be hard on ourselves—we look at the negatives, not the positives. So, take some time to highlight your strengths and then remember to use those strengths throughout your healing process. Take a minute to jot down your strengths. I encourage you to come up with a minimum of three strengths. In case you are struggling to come up with your strengths, here is a short list of examples:

- Humor.
- Trustworthiness.
- Creativity.

- Discipline.
- Patience.
- Kindness/caring.

Exercise: Strengths

1. _____

   _____

   _____

2. _____

   _____

   _____

3. _____

   _____

   _____

Identified Problem/Goals

Finally, we have arrived at the reason you picked up this book in the first place. Why are you looking into therapy, self-help, growth, and healing? Do you have a problem to work on? What is that problem? Sometimes answering these questions is straightforward. Sometimes, however, you don't know the answer—other than that you are feeling unhappy, stuck, "off," etc. That's okay. But the first step is narrowing down the problem. Often, what we label as the identified problem (what we therapists call the "IP") isn't even the *real* problem. Perhaps you know deep inside what the real problem is, but you are in denial. Denial can be powerful—and deceptive. Or maybe the problem you can identify is just the tip of the proverbial iceberg—the real problem lies below the surface, and it's been growing for some time.

In the coming pages, I will lay out some strategies to help you narrow down the real issue. Sometimes, when you step onto a healing path, you might already know (subconsciously) what the problem is, but you just can't put your finger on it consciously. Then a therapist or life coach asks you the right questions and in answering them, you learn more about yourself. Those underlying problems you have been avoiding come to the surface and become crystal clear so you can deal with them, once and for all.

For now, we are just building the foundation for your healing and growth. So, let's start by listing the problem(s) that led you here. Push "Pause." Take time to fill out the My Problems Exercise below. Simply make a list of all that you are struggling with. Take your time. Be vulnerable with yourself. Don't judge yourself.

WAIVER REMINDER

The author of this book is not dispensing medical advice or prescribing the use of any technique as a solution for physical, emotional, or medical problems. Please seek the advice of a physician or other qualified healthcare professional for any medical or psychological situation. The author intends to offer general information and skill-building techniques to help you in your quest for emotional and spiritual well-being. If you use any of the information in this book, neither the author nor the publisher assumes responsibility for your actions.

A NOTE FROM THE AUTHOR

I want to take a moment to acknowledge that when we dig in and face ourselves, we are walking into the possibility of getting triggered by past hurt and pain that has been unresolved. As you move through your journey, if you begin to get triggered at any point, I want you to turn to the skills I share with you and the support you need from outside professional sources.

If you begin to feel triggered, please STOP, put the book down, and refer to your list of professional resources, coping skills, or supports you have created.

If you feel highly triggered, have suicidal thoughts, or do not trust yourself to keep yourself safe, call 911, go to an emergency room, or contact the National Suicide Prevention Lifeline 800-273-8255, which is available 24 hours.

Exercise: My Problems

1. _____

_____

_____

2. _____

_____

_____

3. _____

_____

_____

4. _____

_____

_____

5. _____

_____

_____

If you wrote down your problems (and didn't just think about them), good work! That time and effort show that you believe you're worth the work it takes to heal and grow. If you didn't write down your problems ... C'mon! Pull it together. Go back and do it. You're worth it. I'll wait.

Okay, once you've listed the problems that are bothering you or holding you back, prioritize them. Put them in order. What do you want to resolve first? What do you need to resolve first? The priority should be the one that bothers you or interferes with your life the most. Go ahead ... go back to the Problem's Exercise. Prioritize your list by writing numbers next to each item.

Now, based on the problems you have listed, make a separate list of your goals in the space below. What would you like to get from therapy (or in this case, from this book)? Some examples could include: "I'd like to experience less anxiety;" "I'd like to quit drinking;" "I'd like a healthier marriage;" "I'd like to feel happier;" "I'd like to get over an ex;" "I'd like a promotion at work;" etc. Push that "Pause" button again. Take a minute to review the problems you listed above, then determine what your goals are. If you struggle to come up with your goals, try asking yourself the miracle question listed below.

Exercise: Goals

1. _____

_____

_____

2. _____

_____

_____

3. _____

_____

_____

4. _____

_____

_____

5. _____

_____

_____

Exercise: Miracle Question

Imagine that you go to bed tonight and while you are sleeping, a magic fairy comes to visit you. She waves her magic wand and creates a miracle just for you. When you wake up, your problems are gone. Life is perfect. What is different in your life from yesterday to today? List your answers below.

_____

_____

_____

_____

Do your goals and problems coincide? Did your goals lead you to realize that a problem exists that you didn't list? Examine the correlations or any disconnects in your two lists. Maybe this means reprioritizing. Maybe you need to sit on this for a day or two. Maybe you need to talk it out with a friend or family member. Narrow these things down. A good therapist will ask the right questions to help you get to the core of the issue. Take some time to write down new or additional thoughts about your problem and/or goals. See if you can't get more specific.

_____

_____

_____

_____

Once you have a good idea of the real problems you are dealing with, I want to know some history and details about them. How long have you been dealing with these issues? In what ways? How have you tried to fix these problems? When did you notice they were present in your life? Or, when did they seem to disappear?

So, for example, if you are dealing with anxiety, how do you know it's anxiety? That may seem like a strange question, but as I mentioned earlier, mental health symptoms can be tricky—many different mental health diagnoses can share a lot of the same symptomology, making it hard to pull one apart from the other.

So, back to anxiety. What leads you to believe it's anxiety? Maybe you've noticed racing thoughts, stress, and worry that you just can't let go of. Maybe you struggle to fall asleep at night. Maybe you have shortness of breath or your heart beat is fast. How severe are your symptoms? Have you experienced panic attacks? If so, how often do they occur?

Another example: Perhaps you come to see me because you want to work on anger issues. I'd ask you to describe what your anger looks like. How would I know you're angry? Maybe you keep it all in and it comes out in short, snappy comments to your spouse. Or, at the other extreme, maybe you're throwing things, breaking things, and cursing your spouse out. There is a big difference between the two, and it helps to get a picture of what we are working with.

Review the three paragraphs above and fill in some more detailed information about the history of the problems you listed. Write down anything that comes up for you in the space below.

_____

_____

_____

_____

When do you notice the symptoms of your problem arising? What triggers these symptoms? Going back to the example of anxiety, perhaps you only experience it when you are in a social gathering. Or perhaps you feel anxious every evening before you go to bed, or every morning on your way to work. Can you recall the first time you experienced anxiety? Perhaps it was when you were seven years old and Mom and Dad were fighting over Dad's drinking every other night. Or perhaps it was after a bad car accident when you were fifteen. We want to know if it was a Big "T" Trauma or a little "t" trauma that led to the anxiety.

Since the problem (or problems) you listed above are the reason(s) you are reading this book in the first place, this chapter may feel short or incomplete. Remember, however, we are setting up a solid foundation so you can be prepared to dive deep into healing and growth. So, right now, we need to set this on hold. We'll return soon, when we have more information and when you are better prepared.

NOTES

NOTES

NOTES

NOTES

NOTES

> *Your mind, emotions and body are instruments*
> *and the way you align and tune them*
> *determines how well you play life.*
> —Harbhajan Singh Yogi[1]

Chapter 5
THE MIND / BODY / SPIRIT CONNECTION

As a clinician and in life in general, I take a holistic approach to the wellbeing of my clients, my friends and family, and myself. I pay close attention to mind/body/spirit and aim to get these aspects of being human as much in balance with—and as connected with—each other as possible. The idea/belief that all three facets of life are interconnected and can influence each other is known as "the mind/body/spirit connection."

We can see and experience this connection in different ways. When everything is going well in our lives, for example, we feel great. Our mind, body, and spirit all work in tandem—life flows freely, and we have few worries. When things aren't going smoothly, however, we can feel "out of sorts," anxious, or stressed. Physical complaints may arise and while the symptoms can be real, sometimes nothing shows up on a doctor's tests. That's a good indicator that there is a disconnection between the mind, the body, and the spirit.

---

[1] Harbhajan Singh Yogi, https://www.azquotes.com/.

Stress, especially, can interrupt the balance and affect the flow of our day-to-day experience. I know firsthand how stress and anxiety can lead to physical symptoms. For example, I've experienced stress-induced hives, and I've had intense jaw pain from clenching my teeth because of stress—and even chipped a tooth by clenching my jaw in my sleep! If I experience symptoms like these, I've learned that it's in my best interest to stop what I'm doing, figure out where my thoughts are, what the source of the stress/anxiety might be—and then address it. Generally, what I mean by *address it* is that I've got to stop and be still enough to feel the feelings. I have to sit still enough to identify the thoughts and feelings that are bubbling up. If I give it that time and attention, I can then address it.

The Mind Connection

So, let's break this down. When we say "mind" in this mind/body/ spirit connection, what are we talking about? If you want to know if your mind is in balance or in a healthy place, pay attention to your thoughts. Are your thoughts good, positive, and healthy? Are you challenging your brain? Are you reading? Are you learning? Overall, how is your mental health? What topics are your thoughts on? Are you able to regulate your emotions? Your thoughts are powerful: What you think leads to what you feel and to how you see certain situations and life in general.

An example of the power of our thoughts is the so-called "self-fulfilling prophecy theory." The theory is that if you hold a belief strongly enough for long enough, it will become reality because you have been acting as though what you believe is already true. This is also known in New Thought philosophy as the "Law of Attraction"—thoughts become things. The idea is that our reality is constructed on our thoughts, so, if we think it, we feel it, and we live it.

If you can't pinpoint your thoughts and evaluate your state of mind, try instead to explore your mood. What have your moods been like over the past few weeks? Are you mostly happy, or are you sad, angry, or lonely? Your moods reflect your thoughts directly. To figure out your thoughts, work backward. Can you see a pattern in your moods?

If you can't recall your moods, look at your behaviors. Your behaviors reflect your moods, so ask yourself: "Am I being social? Am I isolating? Am I overreacting or angry? Am I lashing out? Am I self-medicating? Am I being productive or lazy?" Assessing your behaviors will show you where your moods are. Again, work backward: behavior to emotion to thought.

Use the space provided below to make notes that will help you evaluate your mind state.

Once you've evaluated your thoughts, your mood, and your behavior, and you've seen how potent these "mind-connection" aspects of the self can be, you're ready to turn your attention to the next pillar: the body.

_____

_____

_____

_____

_____

_____

_____

The Body Connection

Even though the body is listed as the second pillar in the mind/body/spirit connection, taking care of the body is usually the first "homework assignment" I give my clients in the therapy process. I'll ask, "What are you eating? How are you sleeping? How much are you exercising?" If you are not doing well in these areas, then you may be fighting a losing battle—or at the very least, your progress will be slower and more difficult. Do a little research and you'll discover that sometimes diet and exercise can improve depression and anxiety better than any psychiatric medication.

Let's start with diet: What foods are you putting into your body? Are you providing yourself with the nutrients you need to feel good and stay energized? Or, are you clogging your system up with heavy, processed foods? What we eat has a huge impact on our mood and our energy levels. Anyone who has ever worked hard to cut sugars or fast food out of their lives will attest to the fact that eating fast, processed foods is akin to clogging up the pipes in your home plumbing ... everything gets backed up, things don't get processed properly, and eventually you have a mess. The right foods help your pipes flow properly and keep you functioning like a well-oiled machine. There is a lot of information out there about which foods help with which issues and although it's hard work, it's worth treating your body right.

Next on the body-care list is sleep. When you get good sleep, you allow your body and brain to heal and reboot. It's like plugging your cell phone in at night to recharge—your body needs to reboot and revitalize. I remind my clients to aim for seven to nine hours of sleep every night. Ideally, to develop a healthy circadian rhythm, it's helpful to wake up at the same time every morning and go to sleep at the same time every night. The sleep-wake circadian rhythm affects hormone release, eating habits and digestion, body temperature, and other important bodily functions—so it's important to stay regular.

Many people struggle with sleep, and if that is the case with you, before we go deeply into therapy, we will set aside time to assess your sleep hygiene and work on getting you into a good sleep pattern. I think many people underestimate how much sleep affects our daily lives— for better or for worse. Some people believe they are "functioning just fine, thank you" on four to five hours of sleep a night, but in many cases, they're actually functioning at about seventy-five percent of their potential. They've just gotten used to what that level of "normal" feels like for them. They don't realize that with just a couple more hours of sleep, they could function even better. Only around five percent of the population can function well off of less than six hours of sleep.[2] There are countless benefits to consistently having a good sleep, and that's why it's high on the list of the "self-care for your body" habits we'll work on.

Finally, we are to exercise. Are you doing any? I am by no means saying that you need to be in the gym 7 days a week for 2 hours at a time, but if you are currently not getting any regular physical activity, we will want to start somewhere. I like to encourage my clients to ease into their workouts, taking baby steps slowly so that they do not get frustrated and throw in the towel a week into it. If you already have a work out routine, fantastic! Keep it up and be proud of yourself for that. If not, let's get started. This will look different for everyone based on their preferences of workouts, their phase in life, and their schedule. Take wherever you are or are not at with your workouts and see if you can just add one thing in a week. Maybe it's a 30 minute walk or a 30 minute yoga class. If that seems hard for your schedule, take it down to 15 minutes. Something is better than nothing and we will slowly but surely build upon this. When you're starting to feel stronger or finding more time in your schedule, then go ahead and add in another day or extra time. Within a matter of a few weeks to a few months, you'll be building your routine and your endurance and you'll be thanking yourself for it. Remind yourself that the starting is the hardest part but that you will quickly be reaping the benefits in mind, body and spirit. Don't forget to have fun with it. It may feel like a chore sometimes, but take the time to figure out what kind of workouts you enjoy and how to make them something that you look forward to. Maybe it's a class setting, maybe it's having a walking buddy where you can chat along the way, whatever it is, make it yours.

---

2   Katherine Harmon, "Rare Genetic Mutation Lets Some People Function with Less Sleep," Aug 13, 2009, https://www.scientificamerican.com/article/genetic-mutation-sleep-less/#:~:text=Sleep%20requirements%20seem%20to%20follow,hours%20of%20sleep%2C%20notes%20Fu.

Once we've sorted out your sleep patterns and you've improved your diet and started an exercise routine that works for your lifestyle, you'll have taken long strides toward balancing your own mind/body/spirit connection. Write about your eating, sleeping, and exercise patterns below.

The Spirit Connection

The last pillar in the mind/body/spirit paradigm is spirit. This is big: It's not as clear or cut and dried as the mind and body links are because "spirit" means different things to different people. For example, "spirit" might mean: a religion, a belief system, a worldview, a passion. It might also mean spirituality, soul, that which makes you *you*, etc. Often when I ask people where they are at with spirit, they either don't know, or spiritual awareness is completely lacking in their lives. If this is the case with a client, I'll use "psychoeducation" to enlighten them about the "spirit" part of the mind/body/spirit connection, what spirit is, and why it plays such a big part in wellness. I don't care if a person's spirituality is based on praying to their morning cup of coffee, or what have you … as long as they have a belief system they feel solid in. When we aren't in tune with our spirit, it's impossible to know who we are. If we don't know what aligning our mind, body, and spirit means or looks like, there is no way, no how that we can connect to ourselves or live our life to the fullest.

When we are disconnected from spirit, often we feel something is missing. Things make little sense. We can feel as though we are on auto-pilot, that there is a void in our lives. Life feels pointless, like there is no purpose, no joy. The unknown feels big and scary. We are anxious and floundering around aimlessly. When we are connected and in tune with our spirit, we have a better understanding of who we are, what makes us who we are, what our worldview is, what brings us joy, and what our purpose is. Knowing these things helps us sleep better at night. If, for example, my life perspective is that "whatever is meant to be will be, by the grace of some higher power" and if I am firm in this belief, then I will experience less anxiety. I can fall back on that conviction and be reassured that "I can let things be instead of forcing things along."

Every individual's spiritual path is highly personal, and everyone has a different spiritual journey. But it is vital for our wellbeing that we have a spiritual belief system … whatever it may be. Use the space provided below to make notes about your spiritual journey.

_____

_____

_____

_____

_____

_____

_____

Healthy Thinking

Just as holding a spiritual worldview is crucial to our health and wellness, so too is healthy thinking—that is, thinking in a manner that benefits us and promotes our wellbeing. Let's take a moment to address the concept of "thinking errors." While I don't typically go over this in a client assessment, it is something I watch for in the beginning of every client-therapist relationship.

Thinking errors—or unhealthy thinking styles—are developed patterns of thought that shape our worldview. While you might think that the thoughts that run through your head are benign (because you know your own mind), in fact, we all benefit by keeping our thoughts in check and on track, because if we let negative thoughts run wild in our minds, these "thinking errors" (or "distorted thoughts") can prove not only unhelpful but unhealthy. Some psychologists believe that such distorted thinking is associated with many mental health problems.

If I notice a client falling into an unhealthy thinking style, it's helpful to identify this, bring it to the client's awareness, and work on it by challenging the thoughts regularly. Some common unhealthy thinking styles include: all-or-nothing thinking, overgeneralizing, disqualifying the positive, jumping to conclusions, magnifying or minimizing, making "should" statements, labeling or mislabeling, personalizing or blaming, and applying mental filtering or emotional reasoning. I won't explain each of these, but I encourage you to look them up, learn about them, and figure out which one (or ones) you fall into. Challenging unhealthy thinking styles can change your perspective in life for the better, every time.

If you've gotten to this section of the chapter and you're thinking that the mind/body/spirit connection sounds like a bunch of hippie dippy stuff, I don't blame you, but I encourage you to check out the science behind it. If you do a simple google search, I suggest typing in "The three brains: the head, heart, and gut." This is the scientific language for mind/body/spirit. What resonates with me the most when I read about and look into the head, heart, and gut connection is the suggestion that these three brains are the reason we may often struggle with decisions.

In particular, what I hear myself or my clients saying is something like, "My head says one thing, but my heart tells me another." This is a clear indicator that we are not balanced and connected well in all three areas—they are at odds with each other and leading us in different directions. Some people may go with what their head says. Others may go with what their heart says. Either way, we don't make our best decisions in life until these three brains are all pointing us in the same direction. Have you ever had someone tell you how they knew they were in love with someone or they knew which house was the right one to buy because "I just knew. It just felt right."? This is likely because their mind/body/spirit were all in alignment; there was no second guessing ... doubt was not bubbling up.

You might wonder why science calls it the "three brains." To me, this is the empowering and fascinating part. Each part—the head, heart, and gut—all have their own intrinsic nervous system. This means they've got neurons and can receive, process, store, and adapt information. A short way to say that is that each system can learn. How exciting is that?! We can teach each area to function better. It's like knowing that you can take yourself and create a "Me 2.0" by teaching your mind/body/spirit connection to function better and integrate.

Since you're reading a self-help book, I'm guessing you dig the idea of creating a better version of yourself. It's true that people don't change very much easily. But when we know what areas to work on in our lives, we have a better chance of making real change, and that's a reason to be hopeful.

I mentioned earlier that someone might be more prone to choosing their head over their heart, or their heart over their gut, etc. Why is this? It's the same reason we may feel optimistic or pessimistic about a particular situation—because each area is a neural network (which means it builds upon itself). Think "practice makes perfect." The more you trust your gut, the more it becomes second nature. The more you tell yourself a negative thought, the more of a negative thinker you become. Each time you use one over the other, you create neural pathways that grow each time you use them. When we don't balance these nervous systems out, we create a clash, which shows up as stress. Eventually, we see that we keep making the same mistakes over and over. We wonder: "Why don't I learn?"

In summary, we make better decisions, from a place of our higher consciousness, when we understand the mind/body/spirit connection and know how to make sure we are operating to the best of our ability in each area.

NOTES

NOTES

NOTES

NOTES

NOTES

> *As you sow in your subconscious mind, so shall you reap in your body and environment.*
> —Joseph Murphy[1]

Chapter 6
IDENTIFYING THE NEGATIVE/LIMITING BELIEF BEHIND YOUR PROBLEM

Here we are—at the turning point you've all been waiting for! If you've gotten this far, hopefully you've put a considerable amount of time into assessing and fine-tuning multiple areas of your life. You've laid the foundation you need in order to ground yourself. You've built the framework you need so you can "level up." You've worked on your eating, sleeping, and exercise habits, you've scanned your environments, you've rallied your support systems, and you've gained some coping skills. Good job. This was all hard work—and you did it. Don't stop now.

Remember that problem you identified? What pattern do you keep repeating? What keeps you down? What stops you from moving forward? It's time to dig deeper. We want to understand what's underneath that problem. You identified the problem through your conscious mind; now we want to step down, into your subconscious mind. We want to

---

[1] Joseph Murphy, *The Power of Your Subconscious Mind* (Radford: Wilder Publications, 2007).

figure out what's at the core of your problem, and where it originated. We want to define the core negative or limiting belief that blocks you, subconsciously, from solving your current problem and from jumping to the next level in life. It's time to put a label on what keeps you stuck. You've got to name it to tame it, right?

If identifying your core negative or limiting belief sounds heavy (or even scary), you're not alone. It is heavy, because that belief runs deep. It's something you've avoided subconsciously or that you've suppressed for most of your life. Your negative core belief (or one of them, anyway) may have developed when you were very young—it compounded slowly, and over time, it snowballed to where you are at today. That's a lot to unpack. It's not your fault that you've avoided it; it's natural to not want to feel negative feelings.

We all avoid—in many different ways. All that matters right now is that you're here, ready to face it. Congratulations! That's something to be proud of. *Seriously*. Many people go through their entire lives (or a significantly large portion of their lives) avoiding these core beliefs and holding themselves back in major areas. The average age of someone who comes into my office ready to dig into this stuff is somewhere between the ages of twenty-eight and forty-two. Since the human brain isn't fully developed until around age twenty-five, it makes sense that people gain insight into their patterns after that point. However, the sooner you take a look at this stuff, the sooner (and the longer) you can live a mindful life that brings you joy. It may be scary to address this long-avoided issue, but what's scarier is living the rest of your life on repeat, making the same mistakes, doing unhealthy things repeatedly— staying stuck in the same place and limiting your joy in this life.

It may be scary to face your issues,

but it's scarier to stay stuck and limit your joy.

Let's get to it.

First, we need to label your problem. So, for the sake of an example, I'll tell you about a client that came in to my office and just rocked the

EMDR process. This client, a successful man in his mid-thirties (we'll call him Josh) was hesitant about the whole therapy process. But he was at a place in his life where he didn't know where else to turn. He was baffled by his issue and desperate to change. For the first time in his life, Josh was experiencing severe anxiety from (what seemed to him to be) out of nowhere. He described being on the verge of a panic attack when he left the house or when everything was silent late at night. Even driving could give him a surge of panic. This was a huge problem, as he had to drive and travel often for work. This caused him to lose sleep, stay at home, and cancel hanging out with friends and attending work-related events. He did not perform at his best at work, he avoided people, and he experienced physical symptoms such as a racing heart, shortness of breath, and tense muscles. This was confusing for him, as, in general, he was doing pretty well in life. He owned his own business, made great money, had a wonderful and supportive family, and overall, he was happy.

So, what was going on with Josh? As therapists, we identify a problem based on what is impeding a client's life at the present time. With Josh, I labelled the problem as "anxiety" because at that moment, anxiety was getting in the way of his life.

Let's bring it back to you. What's your problem? Is it anxiety, work, relationships, getting over an ex, stress? You can keep it vague (like in those examples) or you can label your problem specifically, such as saying, "I'm fighting with my husband." Once you've pinned down your problem, we are ready to figure out your negative belief.

There is more to pinpointing a negative belief than you might think. We want to make sure we get to the core negative belief for your issue. We want to make sure it resonates with you in your mind and in your body so that when you allow yourself to think about it and really feel it, it rattles your spirit (and not in a good way). What do I mean by that? How does one pick their negative belief by tapping into mind, body, and soul? Well, everyone moves through this process in a different way, but most people try initially to use their mind (their conscious thought) to pick their problem—but they overthink it. Let's experiment with this and see what you do.

Okay. Think about your problem. In the space below, write down what you would say to me if you were sitting in my office right now. While you think about your problem, tell me what that problem makes you feel about yourself. So, for example:

"Carrie, when I think about my anxiety, it makes me feel like I am

_____

_____

(fill in the blank)."

In the space provided below, list all the negative beliefs you come up with. Most people come up with a minimum of three, but on average, I see five to seven negative beliefs on clients' lists. Don't feel bad if you have more than that. That's not uncommon.

Okay, so perhaps you got one negative belief ... perhaps you got five ... or you didn't get any. Don't worry. Like I said, this isn't as easy as it sounds. Did you say something like "It makes me feel sad ... angry ... frustrated?" That's a great start, but that's not a belief about yourself. That's a feeling you are experiencing.

If that happened and you ended up with just a feeling, feel into that feeling ... and dig deeper. For example:

"I feel sad when I experience my anxiety because it makes me feel like I am

_____

_____

(fill in the blank)."

Okay, great. Take some time. Make a list of as many negative beliefs about yourself around your problem that you can come up with:

Negative Belief Exercise

"When I think about _____(my problem),
it makes me feel like I am:

1. _____

2. _____

3. _____

4. _____

5. _____

6. _____

7. _____

8. _____

9. _____

10. _____

Good work. I want to come back to the idea of integrating mind, body, and spirit. As I mentioned, many people use their conscious mind on this exercise. They overthink it; they struggle. For example, they may land on a negative belief such as "I'm not good enough" but then struggle to resonate with that, or struggle to feel it's true because cognitively, consciously, they know they are good enough. They can write on paper all the reasons they are good enough, such as "I have a great family, friends, career, car, home." However, we don't want you to stay in your cognitive mind because what you know in your conscious mind and what you feel/believe on the inside can be two very different things.

You may know you're good enough, but deep inside you might not believe it to your core. You know it, but you don't feel it. Your conscious mind might be good at telling you repeatedly that you're good enough … which is a great skill. However, we don't operate our lives from our conscious minds. So, no matter how much your conscious mind tells you, loud and clear, that "You are good enough," your actions are being directed from your subconscious operating system. So, we want you to pick your negative belief based on what you feel in your heart and body—not what you think in your head.

"Great, Carrie," you're thinking. "So how do I figure out what's going on in my heart and body?"

Good question. Stay with me. Let's keep plugging away at this. It's important. What do you *feel*? How can you know what you feel when all you can hear is your conscious mind talking to you? We'll get to that step, but first let's explore your negative belief options even further. Let's make sure we are covering all our bases here. This is where I pull out my handy dandy Negative Cognitions List for you to ponder. No matter where you are, and whether you have none, one, or ten negative beliefs written down, we want to double check: Are you digging deep or are you staying at the surface level?

Take a moment to read through the list below and check out the additional list at this URL: https://www.instituteforcreativemindfulness.com

While you read, keep your problem in your mind. Otherwise, you might delve into other areas of your life and come up with negative beliefs unrelated to the problem at hand. At any given time in our life, we can walk around with multiple problems. Just focus on this one for now.

So again … back to the list. Focus on your problem as you read through the list. Notice: Which negative beliefs resonate with you? If something resonates, circle it or write it down on a piece of paper.

Negative Cognitions List

- I should have known better.

- I should have done something.
- I did something wrong.
- I am to blame.
- I cannot be trusted.
- My best is not good enough.
- I cannot trust myself.
- I cannot trust anyone.
- I am in danger.
- I am not safe.
- I cannot show my emotions.

Please do take the time check out the URL above for more negative cognitions for your consideration as pinpointing the most accurate one at the very core of the issue is important. Or, you can find a similar list at: https://www.psychologytools.com/resource/emdr-cognitions/ Maybe check out both lists.

Okay. Good work. Hopefully you've got at least one negative belief now, if not many. If you have multiple negative beliefs, great, we can work with that. Now we need to narrow it down to one. This is where we will pull in the mind/body/spirit again, to figure out which one is *your One.* I like to do this by a process of elimination. If you were sitting in my office with me, I would have you close your eyes while I read the negative beliefs back to you, two by two. I'd have you close your eyes because I want you to note how you feel physically in your body when you hear the words. I want you to keep the one that hits you the hardest in a negative way. Keep the one that feels icky or like a punch to the gut. I want you to cross off the one that didn't have such a strong impact. You will go two by two until you are down to your last one. If you are doing this by yourself, I suggest you do this in front of a mirror. Watch yourself as you read the words out loud. Sometimes it's hard to pick one over the other. In my office, I watch a client's nonverbal reactions carefully while I read this list out loud. When a negative belief hits someone harder, there is often more of a non-verbal physical reaction that shows up, generally in their face. Sometimes it's tears welling up, sometimes it's a wince, or it may be just a glance down to the floor. But when you're watchful, you can pick up on what's different about your reaction to one item on the list than to the others.

Okay, you know what to do ... Go for it! Take some time on this. Allow yourself to feel your physical reactions. Take time to breathe deeply and slowly. Give yourself permission to be honest with yourself. Be open to focusing on your feelings rather than your thoughts. *You've got this.*

How My Problem Came to Be (My Negative Belief Timeline)

Now you've got your negative belief relating to your current problem. Good work! That is no small feat. It's time for our next step in rewiring our brain: The Timeline. Before we do that, let's refer back to Josh for a minute. Remember Josh and his problem with anxiety that seemingly came out of nowhere? The reason that I use the word *seemingly* is that, of course, this anxiety did not pop up out of thin air overnight for no reason. When anxiety hits out of the blue like that, what actually happens is that at a certain stage in life (often in the thirty- to forty-year-old range), we hit a saturation point (some call this a "mid-life crisis" at its most extreme). If you google "saturation point" you will get this:

> "sat·u·ra·tion point /ˌsaCHəˈrāSHən ˌpoint/ *noun* Chemistry noun: saturation point 1. the stage at which no more of a substance can be absorbed into a vapor or dissolved into a solution."[2]

When I use the term "saturation point" regarding our mental health, I'm referring to overflowing our "tea kettle" with all the stuff we've been avoiding, shoving down, and suppressing for most of our life. Basically, we can't take on anymore. There is nowhere for it to go but out. Our minds are infinitely fascinating and they can serve us to our advantage, or absolutely to our destruction. For a while, we can get good at suppressing things we don't like to think about or deal with. We lock those things up deep in our unconscious minds. We like to think they have disappeared magically, that we never have to deal with them

---

[2] https://www.dictionary.com/browse/saturation-point

again. However, there comes a point when we've been shoving down too much stuff for too long. We simply cannot fit any more in—our tea kettle boils over and pours into areas of our lives that seem unrelated. It flows into the strangest places, in the strangest ways, at the strangest times. It can land us with an ulcer, a heart attack ... or in the ER with a panic attack.

I remember as clear as day when I hit my saturation point. I was in my early thirties and my indicator popped up as a physical symptom. For me, it was the tense pain in the jaw and the cracked tooth I mentioned earlier. Remember, the mind/body connection is huge and physical symptoms are important to pay attention to in our lives! Think of physical symptoms as the indicator lights on your car. Assuming your car works properly, we trust that the indicator lights are there for a good reason. If you notice that the "Check Engine" light comes on or the "Empty" light on your gas gauge pops on, do you ignore it and keep going? Most likely not—unless you like to walk on the wild side and risk breaking down. If we ignore those indicator lights, we end up causing more damage than if we had paid attention. The car is your body, and your symptoms are the indicator lights. Pay attention to them and save yourself some pain, struggle, and money.

Core issues rarely come out of "nowhere." Ignore them long enough, and eventually, they will resurface ... with a vengeance. Therefore, let's figure out just how long your core beliefs have been around and where they started.

So, back to Josh. He came to my office to deal with anxiety and narrowed his negative belief down to "I'm not in control" (that's a common belief for anxiety, by the way). Now to the timeline. I guided Josh to scan through his life, chronologically, to find times where there were significant memories or events in which he felt "I'm not in control."

This can be related to anything in life; it doesn't have to be related just to anxiety. Some people come up with only three to four experiences on their timeline, but most people come up with ten or more. Some people stay perfectly on track and go chronologically year to year, some may jump around (that's okay), some may struggle to remember. If someone is struggling, I will go through major life stages one by one. For example, I'll ask what they remember in their toddler years, their elementary days, middle school days, high school days, after graduation, then maybe college, career and work, and whether they can tap into any memories of that feeling with friends, family, dating relationships, etc.

Some experiences may look something like this: "When I was in elementary school, we had to move to a new house and school, and I didn't want to. I hated the new school. There was nothing I could do." Or "In middle school, a group of friends all ganged up on me and then excluded me. In high school I was in a car accident. My step-dad was extremely strict my entire life." Or maybe it was something like, "My parents divorced when I was twelve, and my dad moved across the country."

There is no right or wrong to these memories. These memories are yours. They can seem small or big to you. It doesn't matter. All that matters is how they made you feel. If they struck the chord of your negative belief, write it down.

So, now it's your turn. Take some time to go through your timeline. You may even want to do your timeline, set it down, and come back to it another day and see if a new memory resurfaces.

Exercise: The Lifespan of My Problem

Times in My Life When I Felt (*Insert Negative Belief*).

Toddler years:

_____

_____

_____

Elementary school:

_____

_____

_____

Middle school:

_____

_____

_____

High school:

_____

_____

_____

College or after graduation/twenties:

_____

_____

_____

In work experiences:

_____

_____

_____

With friends:

_____

_____

_____

With family:

_____

_____

_____

Others:

_____

_____

_____

Significant dating relationships/Marriages:

_____

_____

_____

Good work! You've got your timeline.

Try not to place any judgments on your timeline. It's okay if it's just a few experiences, and it's okay if it's five pages worth of experiences. It's okay if the experiences seem silly or if they're memories you'd forgotten for years. They're yours, and they matter to you for different reasons, and that's all there is to it. These memories, no matter how big or small, or how silly or traumatic (or whatever they may seem to you), have formed the core negative belief for the problem you are focusing on. Remember, you can have more than one negative belief that you operate from in your life, but to start, narrow it down to one negative belief that pertains to your problem. This will be your accessing "incident" through the "reprocessing phase." We'll get to that in a while.

When I am in session with a client, I want to make sure they step out of their rational, conscious brain ... and *feel*. I ask my client to lean back on the couch, relax, and close their eyes. Just as we did with the negative belief process, I ask them to listen as I read each memory back to them and to notice how they feel in their body. I ask them to pick the memory that feels the worst ... like a punch in the gut when they hear it.

Obviously, if you are reading through the timeline by yourself, you can't close your eyes. So, read them one at a time, slowly. Jot down the physical feelings or emotions that surface. Or, just like we did with the negative belief, do the "process of elimination." Read them two by two and with each pair, cross off the one that's the least disturbing.

When you land on your strongest memory/experience, we refer to this as your "Incident."

My final core negative belief Incident for my current problem of _____ is:

_____

_____

_____

Now we have your core negative belief and your incident. We know what is underneath your current problem (on some level). For example, let's go back to Josh for a moment. Josh's problem isn't just anxiety—as if it's this big mysterious thing that occurs within him for no reason—Josh's anxiety spikes when he feels "I'm not in control." After identifying his timeline and incident, we know that Josh's belief system of "I'm not in control" originated (or at least was compounded in his belief system) when he was ten years old. His parents divorced, he endured years of emotional abuse from a step-parent, and his biological parent did not protect him.

So, for Josh, anxiety isn't his true problem. It is the problem that he came to therapy for, but now we see that his true problem is a belief system of "I'm not in control." He has been operating his life around that belief and has hit a saturation point. I hear myself saying this over and over in therapy sessions: The "problem" we notice is not the real problem—it is the identified symptom of a deeper problem.

When I work with couples, I often use the following example of *a problem* not being *the problem*: Imagine that a couple (let's call them "Jim and Jane") is fighting over a huge pile of dishes in the sink. The argument blows up. Suddenly, they stop talking to each other for three days. Over dishes. Really? Dishes? Are they truly upset about the dishes? No. The dishes are the identified problem, but what's the belief under the dishes issue? Jane might think, "I have to do everything around here. Jim takes me for granted all the time." These thoughts are swirling around one of Jane's negative core beliefs—something like, "I'm not loveable." At first glance those thoughts and that negative core belief may not seem to line up, but that's why we have to dig in and double check. On the surface, Jane may blame Jim for the fight over the dishes, but subconsciously Jane might think, "If Jim loved me enough, he wouldn't ignore me when I ask him to do the dishes."

Jim, on the other hand, may think something like, "I planned to do the dishes later. Just because they're not done the way Jane wants when she wants doesn't mean I won't do them. She's so controlling." Jim's negative core belief might be something like, "I'm not in control." So, Jim is sensitive to and triggered by anything in his life that feels like a loss of control or being controlled.

Again, the "presenting problem" is rarely "the problem." This is where, instead of talking in code about the dishes (because the dishes aren't the real issue), it's beneficial to understand our "stuff," identify our thoughts and feelings, and use "I" statements to express them. For example, instead of coming home, seeing the dishes piled up, and saying "Jim, you're such a jerk. Why do you always leave a mess for me to clean up?" with practice, Jane could learn to say "It may not be intentional, Jim, but when I see the dishes left undone, I feel like you expect me to clean up after you. I feel taken for granted and unlovable."

Most likely (not always—but especially at first) Jane will get a different response from Jim when she makes an "I feel..." statement, as opposed to making a "You always..." statement. To be genuine and transparent in a relationship, we have to know ourselves well enough to show the other person who we are. Otherwise, we are walking around showing our loved one who we wish we were—and in essence, we are living a lie. Since we are happiest when we are being our authentic selves, it is worth the journey to figure out who that person is.

**To be genuine in a relationship,
we have to know who we are.**

In the paragraph above, I said that your partner is most likely to respond differently to the latter two "I feel..." statements, but not always at first. I say "not always at first" because when one partner changes, the dynamic of the relationship changes. Here, for example, when Jane expresses her feelings, Jim can become defensive because their "song and dance" is changing. Remember we talked earlier about the identified patient/ problem (the IP). Well, in this scenario, for Jim, Jane's new way of communicating her feelings can trigger Jim into feeling that his IP is Jane herself. Jim's not in step with Jane's new way of relating ... the homeostasis is changing. Earlier, I touched upon homeostasis briefly, but it deserves more discussion. According to http://www.healthofchildren. com/E-F/Family-Therapy.html:

HOMEOSTASIS (BALANCE) Homeostasis means that the family system seeks to maintain its customary organization and functioning over time, and it tends to resist change. The family therapist can use the concept of homeostasis to explain why a certain family symptom has surfaced at a given time, why a specific member has become the IP, and what is likely to happen when the family begins to change.[3]

All systems (including family systems) operate according to an established process. You and your partner (or whoever) become accustomed to a little "song and dance" that you've created. Just because you've adapted to it doesn't mean it's healthy—it's just what you've come to know and expect from your interactions with each other. There's comfort in familiarity.

Let's consider again the situation illustrated in the 'dishes' scenario above. Let's say that Jane works on herself and uses one of the "I feel..." statements when she shares with Jim what happens when she finds the dishes left undone. Even though we know that Jane's "I feel..." message is kinder, it doesn't mean Jim will receive her message in the intended way. Jim may, for example, react to Jane's tone of voice, her expression, or the way she is standing. He may already have filled in the dialogue of what he expects to hear because Jane and Jim have been here a hundred times before.

I watch this play out with couples in therapy all the time. For example, say Jim and Jane see me and share their years and years of "the same old song and dance." Jim may be so used to hearing Jane say one thing repeatedly that even though that's not what she's saying *this time*, he assumes that's what she'll say, so that's what he hears and that's what he reacts to. So, with the dishes scenario, Jim gets so thrown off by Jane's out-of-character "I feel" statement, he doesn't have time to process it. So, he just pulls out his go-to reaction. How can Jim and Jane change this song and dance?

Often, I warn couples that if they are working hard to make lasting changes, things may get worse before they get better. Even though one person is making healthy changes, it takes consistent change over a long period for homeostasis to find a new pattern.

---

[3] You can read more on this topic at http://www.healthofchildren.com/E-F/Family-Therapy.html#ixzz6gSq6c1Yl.

To give you another example, consider the idea of New Year's resolutions. They rarely work, right? Why? According to a *Times Tribune* article, "Studies show that only 8% of Americans who make a New Year's resolution actually keep them all year and 80% have failed by the start of February."[4] Keeping resolutions is all about our mindset, our thought process, and our negative beliefs. Due to our own internal homeostasis or operating system, it is unlikely we will change into a different person or adopt a different way of operating overnight.

Let's take working out at the gym as an example of our New Year's resolution. Pretty common, right? There can be some strong negative beliefs around working out. Maybe a subconscious negative belief such as "I can't be successful" holds you back from meeting your workout goals. You can take steps behaviorally to meet your goal—and it may work for a while. For example, if you haven't worked out in two years and you want to change your homeostasis, instead of setting a goal of working out for two hours a day, every day of the week, starting tomorrow, you have a better chance of seeing lasting changes if you take baby steps, adjust to the changes slowly, and not shock your system. You also have a far, far better chance of seeing lasting changes if you have worked on your negative core belief first. Remember: thoughts → feelings → actions.

When my clients come to me wanting to make drastic changes (such as losing weight or stopping smoking), I walk them through a preferred therapeutic approach—if they will commit to it. First, through EMDR therapy (or a similar therapeutic protocol), I have them work on the negative belief that holds them back. I follow that up with coaching/behavioral plans. Finally, when they are ready to take action, to throw the subconscious mind some additional positive messages, I boost our hard work with tailored hypnotherapy sessions. I ask them either to listen to our recorded session or to pick a YouTube self-hypnotherapy recording they like. Whatever they choose, they commit to listening daily—ideally, twice a day for a month or two. They identify and understand

---

[4] https://www.thetimestribune.com/news/local_news/tips-for-making-sure-your-new-years-resolutions-stick/article_8cd14b54-17fd-51a9-ab5a-89859e6e34c4.html.

their negative beliefs, clear those out, replace them with positive beliefs, and continue to follow through behaviorally by attending to the mind/body/soul along the way.

As I mentioned earlier, the problems we talk about are not the real problems in our lives. We'll always have problems. What makes a problem a bigger or smaller issue for us is how we choose to respond to it. I recall a favorite quote from grad school—I believe it was from family therapists Nichols and Schwartz—they said that people get stuck because they don't recognize how they are participating in their own problem.

If we step back and identify our part in the problem—whether that is two percent or ninety percent—and we are accountable, we have a real chance of doing something about the problem. Of course, that's if the other person is willing to do the same and meet us in the middle. And there's the issue—we can't control what the other person in any interaction will do about their part of the problem. We can only change situations in which we have control.

We will never—I repeat, *never*—have control over other people. For example, people can spend their entire marriages trying to change their spouse. They try, they realize it doesn't work, it backfires, and it leads to divorce. This goes for parenting as well. You might have more wisdom and life experience than your child, but you aren't the expert on them nor can you control them. Why? Because you are not in their brains or bodies. Stop trying to control things you cannot control. You will create bigger problems in your life.

I like to fall back on the verse in the "Serenity Prayer" that's often used in AA. It says:

God grant me the serenity

To accept the things I cannot change;

Courage to change the things I can;

And wisdom to know the difference.[5]

If you're not religious, it still applies—just change out the word "God" with whatever resonates with you. Either way, if we could all adopt and apply this adage consistently in our lives, we would save ourselves a lot of struggles.

[5] Reinhold Niebuhr, "The Serenity Prayer," https://www.hazeldenbettyford. org/articles/the-serenity-prayer

NOTES

NOTES

NOTES

NOTES

NOTES

> *We cannot change anything until we accept it.*
> *Condemnation does not liberate, it oppresses.*
> —Carl Jung[1]

Chapter 7
INSIGHT IS A GREAT FIRST STEP: NOW WHAT?

Application: I Have Identified My Negative Belief. What Now?

Congratulations for getting this far! Good work. Seriously. This stuff isn't easy. It can feel yucky to self-reflect and explore the shadow parts of ourselves that we ignore or deny, that we are ashamed of or don't like, and that make us feel sad and hurt. Give yourself some serious credit for doing it and for sticking with it.

However, you're not done. If you're here, you've examined your timeline and life experiences and you've recognized and labeled your core negative belief around a particular problem. You've gained some great insight, and that's a big deal—but it does not always create lasting change. Sorry. I wish it did. I wish I could tell you that you just have to figure things out; that if you analyze hard enough, and understand it, it all changes. Nope. Not the case. (If it were, I'd have been a guru at

---

[1] Carl Jung, https://www.azquotes.com/.

seventeen years old for all of the things I tried to over-analyze. I know you feel me.) Insight alone does not create change in your life. If it did, knowing cigarettes cause lung cancer would make it easy for people to quit smoking. Knowing that eating healthy food and working out helps us lose weight would make it easy to lose weight. Insight alone does not create change—especially not lasting change. There's more work to be done. Do not give up.

So now what? What's the hard work? The next step that I highly encourage in your self-healing journey is to ask for help and get into therapy to follow through with the healing process to its entirety. It's time to dig in really deep, and this is often best done with some hand holding and in a safe and supported environment.

I know. That was far from being earth-shattering guru wisdom. I'm sure you wanted to hear something like: "You must go on a solo journey to the highest peak of Mount Kailash, meditate for four hours, fast for three days, and sip an Ayahuasca drink made by a local shaman...." You get my point. If you have the time and budget to do that, awesome, do it! Take me with you. It sounds lovely, but it's not *the* answer. There is no one answer for everyone. This is your life, your journey, and your experience. The relationship you develop with your therapist will lead you to your answer. Not only will working with a therapist help you to find yourself and heal that much faster, but you will then have your person for all the curveballs that life may throw at you in the future as well. Life is ever-changing, and so are we. Having someone you trust to open up to and share and bounce ideas off of will help you work through all of the ever-changing areas of your life. If it's not one thing, it's the next, right? We are all constant "masterpieces in progress." We are all worth investing the time and energy to check in with our therapist and ourselves on a regular basis.

I have a zillion reasons why it's time at this point to take a break from the self-help for the issue you're working on—but I'll go over just a few of the reasons that pertain to the methodology this book has loosely been following: EMDR therapy.

You have made it through this process on your own. Wow! What a great learning experience. Now it's time to get really honest with yourself. Did you do your very best? Did you maybe cheat a little along the way? Did you dig as deeply as you could? Did you lie to yourself a bit ... or avoid something subconsciously? Don't worry—it's only human to cut corners and make it easy on ourselves. I'll be the first to admit that I cut corners in my life—like when I do workout videos at home. I pride myself on being honest and ethical, but when it comes to working out at home, I am a liar and a cheater. I will cheat out on exercises, doing only six reps instead of ten. I lie to myself, thinking, "That was good enough" or "I did the best I could." I quit and tell myself, "It's okay." Then I wonder why I'm not getting the results I wanted. Hmmm. Hey, I have never claimed to be a track star. But the part of me that comes out when I'm in an exercise class—that's my best me! When I'm in a workout class, I know that there are people watching me, holding me accountable to ten reps instead of six, you can bet I'm going to do it. Accountability! Accountability, connection, and energy! That workout studio mirror and the instructor saying "Good job. Hang in there. I know it's hard, but push through it. You'll thank yourself later," man, that turns my workout results around. Bottom line and moral of the story: I need help to get a good workout for my body. I also need help to get a good workout for my brain, my heart, and my spirit.

It is your therapist's job to guide you to the subconscious thought patterns going on within you and to help you understand those thoughts, feelings, and behaviors. So, your job is to find an EMDR therapist that resonates with you, a therapist that "gets you" and has experience in working with your specific therapeutic issues.

Okay, so once you're in therapy (and if you're following the EMDR track), now is the point in the EMDR process that we are ready for "reprocessing." Settle in. Get ready to rock your therapy. (Actually, this is the part I like to create a "safe space" for, but I'll come back to that in a moment.)

The "reprocessing" part of EMDR is not something I recommend you do on your own. I'm not ruling it out as impossible, but right now my clinical opinion is that it is not best practice. So, what is the reprocessing part of EMDR? This is, as my clients have put it, "the hippie dippy Voodoo magic part." It's the part in which clients see and feel changes within themselves and in their lives that seem to appear out of nowhere, like magic. The reprocessing part of EMDR is when the clinician guides you through letting your brain "zone out" in a way that drowns out your conscious mental chatter (or "monkey mind"). This allows you to tap into your subconscious thought patterns and access the memories and experiences stored there so your brain can heal itself. When your brain has access to these subconscious thought patterns and memories, it will see where the "errors" or "glitches" are and reprocess the experience. It will rewire itself in a healthy way. This helps to diminish negative feelings around your difficult or painful experiences. As the EMDR Institute website says, "EMDR therapy shows that the mind can in fact heal from psychological trauma, much as the body recovers from physical trauma."[2] For example, if you have a cut on your finger, it will heal on its own given you don't allow anything to get inside of it and irritate or infect it. The mind is the same way. If you remove the blocks of suppression, your mind will allow healing to begin.

Not only is your therapist your accountability partner, he or she is holding up a mirror for you while you gaze at your past, while you reflect on painful memories, while you're shaking so hard from emotion that you can't hold that mirror yourself. Your therapist has an energy that mixes with yours to create a relationship dynamic that is more powerful than the sum of its parts. What happens in that exchange is not something you can recreate on your own. Why? Because when you speak to your therapist, you literally hear your own voice say the things—all the things—that you never wanted to hear said inside your own head. You give those thoughts life and presence so you can decide to do something about them instead of shoving them back down. Once your therapist hears them, they're out there. They're on the table. You're held accountable. Then you have something you can work with to create *real change*.

Your therapist will feel your energy. Your therapist will learn your patterns, know what it means when you're quiet, notice when you're

---

2 https://www.emdr.com/what-is-emdr/.

avoiding, know why you're happy, notice when you're withholding, know what your nonverbals mean, what it means when you look down, what it means when you sit forward on the couch, et cetera. Your therapist will catch and highlight things about you that you cannot see. Your therapist will ask the right questions, the hard questions, the inspiring questions. Your therapist will feel like a "safe place" to visit even if you cry through seventy-five percent of your session. Your therapist will call you out in a kind and gentle way when you're avoiding growth or hard work. Your therapist will help create a space where you can be completely, totally, 100% yourself. Your therapist will create a space in which you can "let your hair down" and breathe easily. I could go on and on, but it's one of those "You have to see it to believe it" things.

I believe the relationship created between therapist and client is one of the most important (if not the most important) facilitators of change for the therapeutic process. According to a study by Counselling Psychologist Dr. Lynne M. Knobloch-Fedders, "Since the relationship between the therapist and patient appears so crucial to treatment success, experts have tried to define a 'good relationship.' One pioneering expert, Dr. Edward Bordin, defined a good therapeutic relationship as comprising three essential qualities: an emotional bond of trust, caring, and respect; agreement on the goals of therapy; and collaboration on the 'work' or tasks of the treatment."[3] If you're ready to contact a therapist, I recommend going to www.psychologytoday.com. There you can look at profiles and even filter results by specific topics such as your insurance, preferred treatment (such as EMDR), or other specializations. It's a great resource and makes the search less overwhelming.

As I've mentioned, the therapeutic relationship is key to you making progress in therapy. If you are not connecting to your therapist for whatever reason, try another one. Make sure you find the right fit—don't settle for less. This is your life, your wellbeing, and your mental health. You are trusting your therapist with your deepest, darkest secrets. Make sure you feel safe in the space they provide for you.

---

[3] Lynn M. Knobloch-Fedders, "The Importance of the Relationship with the Therapist," (2008), https://www.family-institute.org/behavioral-health-resources/importance-relationship-therapist.

Oh, one last thing! I told you I would come back to the "safe place." What a lovely note on which to end our time together. Generally, before I jump into any reprocessing with a client, I have them set up their "safe, happy, calm place." I ask my client: "When you are feeling sad, angry, or hurt, or you're having a bad day, if you could snap your fingers and teleport to a place where your negative feelings would disappear and you'd feel safe and calm, peaceful and happy ... where would you go?"

My happy place is the cliché white sandy beach by the ocean. Or, every once in a while, when I am trying to go to my happy place, I catch myself drifting to a small lake a few miles west of my hometown. In high school, a few of us would go there—it seemed like hardly anyone knew about it. It was so quiet and peaceful to take our floaties out on the lake, just two or three of us floating, soaking up the sun in peace and quiet. So, whether it's that lake or a beautiful, white sandy tropical island I drift off to, it's always the water for me.

I know ... it can seem cheesy to close your eyes and imagine going somewhere else, but try it. Imagining your happy place has tremendous power to shift your emotional state—and doing it for just thirty seconds can change your thoughts and mood drastically, at least for a bit.

Once you find your happy, safe place, I encourage you to go there often. When work gets stressful ... When someone just got under your skin ... When the kids won't stop screaming, crying, and fighting ... Take a few seconds, close your eyes, take yourself to your happy place. Take slow, deep breaths. Here's the kicker: Bring all of your senses into the experience. You can't just think about it and call it a day. You have to shut your door or step outside, close your eyes, take slow, deep breaths, and dive in.

So, for example, my safe place is at the beach or lake, right? If I take myself to that lake, what do I see? I see a small lake, trees, sand, a house off in the distance, and a small recreational building near the beach. When I go deeper, I see nothing at all ... I'm floating on the water, eyes closed. I see darkness. I feel the bright sun warming my skin. If I open my eyes, I see a clear blue sky, or I look for my friend to make sure she hasn't fallen asleep or drifted too far away. What do I hear? I hear birds, but that's about it. The peace and quiet is the best part. What do I feel (touch)? I feel the warmth of the sun on my skin, but it's not too hot because I also feel the cool water balancing the temperature. I feel the weightlessness of floating. What do I taste? Generally nothing, but I may have some sips of Gatorade (dark purple). What do I smell? Nature. The fresh air, the earthy scent. As I type this, I'm dreaming of buying my first lake house—the power of pulling in your senses and letting yourself be there is huge!

Go ahead. Try it. Once you find your safe, calm, happy place, you get to take it with you anywhere and everywhere forever. So, one more assignment. I know, you thought you were done. Where's your safe, calm, happy place? Here's what I want you to do....

Exercise: Happy Space

1. Pick your spot.

    Imagine you are sad, mad, lonely or just not having a great day. If you could snap your fingers and instantly teleport to somewhere that puts a smile on your face, makes you happy, calms you down, relaxes you and feels safe, where would that be? It can be somewhere real or imagined.

    a. _____

2. Make sure there are no memories that would end up tainting it when you go there. For example, don't choose a place you went with an ex and had a giant fight.

3. Close your eyes. Take deep breaths and in your mind, take yourself to your spot.

4. Take time with this exercise ... tap into each of your senses and note what you experience in as much detail as possible below:

   a. Sight (What do you see there?):

   _____

   b. Sound (What do you hear?):

   _____

   c. Smell (What do you smell?):

   _____

   d. Taste (Do you have a favorite drink or snack with you?):

   _____

   e. Touch (What do you feel? What sensations, textures, temperatures, etc.?):

   _____

What a perfect note to wrap up on. Enjoy!

❀ ❀ ❀

Next Steps

Congratulations for finishing this book—not just for reading it but for taking the time to self-explore and get to know and understand yourself and for taking the time to understand what therapy can do for you. As I mentioned at the beginning of the book, the work you have done by reading this book is just the beginning—you've taken the basic steps you needed to take. Now you can start building a foundation that will enable you to transform your life, discover who you are, and become who you want to show up as in the world as you move forward.

I encourage you to keep working on yourself. Reach out to a therapist for guidance and commit to building a better you on a regular basis.

Think about it: We don't just get our car oil changed once and then call it good for the rest of the car's life. We get the oil changed regularly—it's standard maintenance and preventative care. We don't just go to the gym once a year and pat ourselves on the back for our hard work. We go to the gym often, ideally three to five times a week. Reading one book won't change your life permanently. You are worth the effort to continue working on *you*!

As a final note, I started this book with my own EMDR therapy experience and sprinkled tidbits about my process throughout. As a conclusion I'd like to inform the world that I am living happily ever after. Just kidding. This isn't a fairytale. However, I am doing well. I am married to my husband of nearly five years. Our twin toddler boys have just turned three years old. I have two great step-children. I own my own business where I get to fulfill my passion and help people every day.

When it comes to the dating struggles I focused on in my original EMDR experience, I'd be lying if I said that I am now perfect, or that I married a perfect man and we have a perfect marriage. That is not real life. I still have my struggles with my negative belief from time to time. I married a man who has his struggles as well. Like all marriages, ours ebbs and flows and has its highs and lows. However, I can say that I have greatly diminished my struggles with my own negative beliefs of "I'm a handful" or "I'm unlovable." Those no longer resonate with me much at all. I have made great strides in knowing my worth and setting my boundaries in my relationships and my marriage—and I thank EMDR for that. I am currently working on clearing out and healing another negative belief that came to my awareness, and I am ready and excited to do so. I have seen the work I put in pay off: in my own happiness, in my ability to set boundaries, in my self-respect, in my friendships, in my family of origin, in my parenting, and in my marriage. All of this success has not happened overnight, but the delayed gratification is worth it. I know life happens. I cannot predict the future. But if I plan to be married to my husband for the rest of my life and want to be the best parent to my kids that I can be, I know I must continue working on myself and healing myself through EMDR and other therapeutic routes for the rest of my life. We get what we give in life. I believe my family and I are worth the hard work it takes to find and continue to cultivate happiness from the inside out. I will show up to do that hard work any time I am called to do so. I hope that you all choose the same for you and yours.

Working on your mind/body/spirit connection is a lifestyle choice. Living a life that you love is worth the effort. Letting go of pain and everything holding you back is worth the effort. Life is far too short. Spend it in the way you want! I wish you luck in finding your perfect EMDR therapist. Have a wonderful journey back to your true self!

NOTES

NOTES

NOTES

NOTES

NOTES

> *You must learn a new way to think before*
> *you can master a new way to be.*
> —Marianne Williamson[1]

---

[1] Marianne Williamson, https://www.goodreads.com/quotes/964239.

Positive reviews from awesome customers like you help others feel confident about Therapizing Themselves too. Could you take 60 seconds to go to your retailer's website and share your happy experiences? We will be forever grateful.

To connect with Carrie Leaf and to get extra resources that will support the healing journey you learned from the book, visit www.CarrieLeaf.com Thank you in advance for helping us out!

Carrie Leaf
www.CarrieLeaf.com

ABOUT THE AUTHOR

Carrie Leaf is currently a practicing psychotherapist and life coach. She holds her undergraduate degree in Psychology with a minor in Sociology from the University of Northern Iowa. She completed her masters degree in Marriage and Family Therapy, graduating top of her class from Iona College. She has been a practicing psychotherapist for over 10 years and working in the psychology field for over 15 years.

Carrie has worked in the field of psychology in a wide variety of settings, which include hospitals, community mental health, youth residential homes, substance abuse, military base, college university, and private practice. She has worked with a wide variety of clients from all ages and around many different identified problems. She has worked with individuals, couples, families, and groups.

Carrie is a mother to two twin toddler boys and a step-mother to their older brother and sister as well. She is a furbaby mom to two boxer dogs. She enjoys working out, exploring her health and fitness journey, staying active, nature and being outdoors, traveling, and trying new things.

Find out more about Carrie Leaf at www.CarrieLeaf.com

There is nothing either good or bad,
but thinking makes it so.[2]
— William Shakespeare

---

[2] William Shakespeare, Hamlet, https://www.goodreads.com/quotes/21959-there-is-nothing-either-good-or-bad-but-thinking-makes.

BIBLIOGRAPHY

Ahmann, Anne. "Happy. Healthy. Home." Accessed November 6 2020. https://www.happyhealthyhomedm.com/about.

C. JoyBell C. Accessed April 1, 2021. https://www.goodreads.com.

EMDR Institute. Accessed November 22, 2020. https://www.emdr.com/what-is-emdr/.

GeneSight Psychotropic. Accessed November 22, 2020. https://genesight.com/.

Hale, Mandy. Accessed April 1, 2021. https://www.goodreads.com/quotes/7604845.

Harmon, Katherine. "Rare Genetic Mutation Lets Some People Function with Less Sleep." 13 August, 2009. Accessed November 15, 2020. https://www.scientificamerican.com/article/genetic-mutation-sleep-less/#:~:text=Sleep%20requirements%20seem%20to%20follow,hours%20of%20sleep%2C%20notes%20Fu.

Harbhajan Singh Yogi. Accessed April 1, 2021. https://www.azquotes.com/.

Jankowski, P. J., and L.M. Hooper, L. M. "Differentiation of self: A validation study of the Bowen theory construct." *Couple and Family Psychology: Research and Practice* 1, no. 3 (2012): 226–243. Accessed November 15 2020. https://doi.org/10.1037/a0027469 and https://psycnet.apa.org/record/2012-05951-001.

Jung, Karl. Accessed April 1, 2021. https://www.azquotes.com/.

Kupferberg, Tuli. https://www.goodreads.com/quotes/57149-when-patterns-are-broken-new-worlds-emerge.

Knobloch-Fedders, Lynn M. "The Importance of the Relationship with the Therapist." 2008. Accessed February 15, 2021. https://www.family-institute.org/behavioral-health-resources/importance-relationship-therapist.

Lipton, Bruce. Accessed April 1, 2021. https://www.brainyquote.com/topics/subconscious-quotes.

Maté, Gabor. Accessed April 1, 2021. https://www.goodreads.com/author/quotes/4068613.Gabor_Mat_?page=4.

Mayo Clinic Staff. "Caffeine: How much is too much?" 6 March, 2020. Accessed December 16, 2020. https://www.mayoclinic.org/healthy-lifestyle/nutrition-and-healthy-eating/in-depth/caffeine/art-20045678.

Mayo Clinic Staff. "Alcohol Use: Weighing Risks and Benefits." 26 October, 2019. Accessed December 12, 2020. https://www.mayoclinic.org/healthy-lifestyle/nutrition-and-healthy-eating/in-depth/alcohol/art-20044551.

McLeod, Saul. "Maslow's Hierarchy of Needs." SimplyPsychology.org. 29 December, 2020. Accessed November 21, 2020. https://www.simplypsychology.org/maslow.html.

Murphy, Joseph. *The Power of Your Subconscious Mind*. Radford: Wilder Publications, 2007.

Niebuhr, Reinhold. "The Serenity Prayer." Accessed March 15, 2021. https://www.hazeldenbettyford.org/articles/the-serenity-prayer.

Shapiro, F. *Eye Movement Desensitization and Reprocessing: Basic Principles, Protocols, and Procedures* (2nd edition). New York: Guilford Press, 2001.

Shakespeare, William. *Hamlet*. Accessed April 1, 2021. https://www.sparknotes.com/nofear/shakespeare/hamlet/page_106/.

Wikipedia. "Transgenerational Trauma." 14 January 2021. Accessed January 8, 2021. https://en.wikipedia.org/wiki/Transgenerational_trauma.

Williamson, Marianne. Accessed April 1, 2021. https://www.goodreads.com/quotes/964239.

URLs (Accessed Between November 15, 2020 – April 5, 2021):

http://www.healthofchildren.com/E-F/Family-Therapy.html#ixzz6gSq6c1Yl.

https://www.alcoholics-anonymous.org.uk/Members/Fellowship-Magazines/SHARE-Magazine/December-2019/The-Serenity-Prayer-and-Me#:~:text=God%2C%20grant%20me%20the%20serenity,wisdom%20to%20know%20the%20difference.

https://www.google.com/search?sxsrf=ALeKk033vxdBwiHGdj8-ot7M_Vs8Kf9kXA:1608306509362&q=Dictionary&stick=H4sIAAAAAAAAAONQesSoyi3w8sc9YSmZSWtOXmMU4-LzL0jNc8lMLsnMz0ssqrRiUWJKzeNZxMqFEAMA7_QXqzcAAAA&zx=1608306560870#dobs=saturation%20point.

https://www.instituteforcreativemindfulness.com.

https://www.psychologytools.com/resource/emdr-cognitions/.

https://www.thetimestribune.com/news/local_news/tips-for-making-sure-your-new-years-resolutions-stick/article_8cd14b54-17fd-51a9-ab5a-89859e6e34c4.html.

www.psychologytoday.com.

Maslow's Hierarchy of Needs. Accessed November 15, 2020. https://www.simplypsychology.org/maslow.html.

Maslow's Hierarchy of Needs, image. Accessed April 6, 2021. https://shutterstock.com.

NOTES

NOTES

NOTES

NOTES

NOTES

NOTES

NOTES

NOTES

NOTES

NOTES

NOTES

NOTES

NOTES

NOTES

NOTES

NOTES

NOTES

NOTES

NOTES

NOTES

NOTES

Made in the USA
Las Vegas, NV
26 December 2021

39416014R00095